ACRES OF DIAMONDS

ACRES
OF DIAMONDS

All Good Things Are Possible,

Right Where You Are,

And Now!

BY

RUSSELL H. CONWELL

THE ONLY COMPLETE TEXT EDITION

Tree of Life Publications

Tree of Life Publications, P. O. Box 126
Joshua Tree, CA 92252
Printed in the United States of America

A new edition, with a new foreword, cover and editing.
Original edition: 1915, Harper & Bros.

ISBN: 0-930852-25-7

Library of Congress Cataloging-in-Publication Data

Conwell, Russell Herman, 1843-1925
    Acres of diamonds: all good things are possible, are
    right where you are, and now! / Russell H. Conwell.
       p. cm.
    "The only complete text edition."
    Edited from 1915 Harper & Bros. ed.; new material
      added by Bianca Leonardo, editor; new subtitle.
    Includes: Conwell's life and achievements/
      by Robert Shackleton
    ISBN: 0-930852-25-7
    1. Success. 2. Conwell, Russell Herman, 1843-1925
    3. Baptists-United States-Clergy-Biography.
    I. Shackleton, Robert, 1860-1923. Conwell's life and
    achievements. 1993.
    II. Title. BJ1611.C543 1993
    248.4--dc20   93-16505
                                              CIP

Russell H. Conwell, in early life

Dedicated

To All Humanity.

May each one of you find your own

"Acres of Diamonds."

Acknowledgements

The editor/publisher is grateful to Lightbourne Images for the exquisite cover on this new edition. Thanks also to Al Gilbert for his excellent typesetting of our books, and for providing the poem "Abou Ben Adhem" from his old elementary schoolbook.

CONTENTS

Part II

THE AUTHOR'S LIFE AND ACHIEVEMENTS,
by Robert Shackleton

★ ★ ★ ★ ★

Foreword

I was familiar with a small booklet entitled *Acres of Diamonds*, for many years. On November 9, 1991, while in the public library of Yucca Valley, California, I surveyed the books on the sale table. ("Non-fiction, 75¢").

With a thrill, I spotted a small, hard cover volume, *Acres of Diamonds*, with 181 pages, and immediately bought it. I read it through from beginning to end that evening, and resolved to republish it, as a tribute to the great author, and a blessing to the reading public. Finding this volume in my local library is in itself an example of the theme in "Acres of Diamonds." It is the complete text, and was published in 1915 by Harper & Brothers. None of the booklet editions contains the complete text. In this edition, we have reproduced (with minor editing), the complete text. The subtitle is new with this edition. A new cover has been created that reflects the inspiration of this great book. The Archives of Temple University, Philadelphia, Pennsylvania, provided the picture of the author.

It is as important to read *about* Russell Conwell in Part II of this complete volume, as it is to read his famous and amazing lecture. He personally gave it over 6,000 times, and raised over $4,000,000 for good causes—helping poor students, financing Temple University and its adjoining hospital, etc.

Surely Russell Conwell lifted the mass consciousness in his time. He brought a realization of possible success, prosperity, and power to his audiences. What a model of virtue he was for those who knew him or heard him speak.

Through this book, he can likewise inspire and bless us. He can be a model of virtue to all of us, and especially to our youth. He is one to pattern ourselves after.

Meet Russell H. Conwell, a self-made man who lived a totally unselfish life, and who opened doors of opportunity to untold millions through his philosophy that "ALL GOOD THINGS ARE POSSIBLE!"

Conwell: Civil War officer; founder of Temple University (starting with one poor, young, ambitious pupil); founder of a hospital; lawyer; minister; orator; author; organizer—who lived many lives in one, because he wasted no time. He worked seven days a week, sixteen hours per day, even when he was crippled with rheumatism in later years, and filled with pain.

He believed that each of us is placed here on earth for one main purpose—to help others.

Now, please enjoy, use and find your own ACRES OF DIAMONDS!

Bianca Leonardo,
Editor/Publisher

OVERVIEW

Russell Herman Conwell
(1843-1925)
Baptist Minister; Founder of Temple University

Conwell was the creator of "Acres of Diamonds," a phenomenally successful lecture he personally delivered over 6,000 times—creating over $4,000,000 in earnings. (In 1993 dollars, worth approximately $145,000,000). All this fortune was given to youth, education, mankind.

Dr. Conwell used the proceeds of this lecture to help finance hundreds of young men through college. Countless numbers were so inspired by the lecture that they gained places among America's most successful people.

This great man lived and worked in an age and in a land that experienced the greatest expansion, growth, change, invention, progress, and expression of human industry ever known in the history of mankind. In no small way, it is believed that Dr. Conwell made a measurable contribution to this great human endeavor. The author, with his tremendous lecture and widespread influence, played his part by inspiring common people to do great things. He awakened the genius that lies dormant in all of us. We wonder: who sat in his audiences, later to become great?

Here are some of the important events in America that happened during the course of his lifetime:

• The opening of the West—the California Gold Rush of 1849, creating the greatest migration in the history of the world, to a specific location—the gold fields of California.

• The Civil War.

- Oil was discovered and brought into use.

- Many useful wonders in inventions: the harnessing of electricity; invention of the light bulb; the telephone and telegraph; the steam engine; the automobile, the airplane, and many more.

- The acquisition of Alaska.

- The Statue of Liberty ("Liberty Enlightening the World"), a gift from France, was placed in New York Harbor, 1886.

- Several new American religions were founded—two of them by women: Christian Science by Mary Baker Eddy (1866-1910), and Seventh-Day Adventism, founded by Ellen G. White, (1827-1915). Founded in America, they spread worldwide.

- The Spanish-American War.

- The greatest immigration to a new land ever in recorded history.

- The Panama Canal built, a great engineering achievement.

- The First World War.

- The movie and film industry founded in the U.S., to become a worldwide influence.

- Russell Conwell served humanity and was a great inspiration to all.

- Via the magic of a book, his rebirth takes place here in this new volume.

We honor this great FRIEND OF MANKIND.

—Editor

AN APPRECIATION

Although Russell H. Conwell's *Acres of Diamonds* have been spread all over the United States, time and care have made them more valuable, and now that they have been reset in black and white by their discoverer, they are to be laid in the hands of a multitude for their enrichment.

In the same case with these gems, there is a fascinating story of the Master Jeweler's lifework* which splendidly illustrates the ultimate unit of power by showing what one person can do in one day and what one life is worth to the world.

As his neighbor and intimate friend in Philadelphia for thirty years, I am free to say that Russell H. Conwell's tall, manly figure stands out in the state of Pennsylvania as its first citizen and "The Big Brother" to its seven millions of people.

From the beginning of his career, he has been a credible witness in the Court of Public Works to the truth of the strong language of the New Testament parable where it says, "If ye have faith as a grain of mustard seed, ye shall say unto this mountain, 'Remove hence to yonder place,' and it shall remove and nothing shall be impossible unto you."

As a student, schoolmaster, lawyer, preacher, organizer, thinker and writer, lecturer, educator, diplomat, and leader of men, he has made his mark on his city and state and the times in which he has lived. A man dies, but his good work lives.

---

*We believe that the writer is referring to Jesus the Christ.

Conwell's ideas, ideals, and enthusiasms have inspired tens of thousands of lives. A book full of the energetics of a master workman is just what every young person needs.

His yoke fellow,

John Wanamaker

His Yoke Fellow,
John Wanamaker
1915

Editor's Note to John Wanamaker's "Appreciation"—

"His yoke fellow"—editor's interpretation:

In earlier times, farmers used draft horses or strong oxen *yoked together* to do the heavy farm work so necessary for a successful farm.

John Wanamaker, creator of the modern department store, was close friends with Conwell, and it is well established that Conwell had a profound effect on Wanamaker's life and brilliant successes. Evidence of their closeness is shown by the fact that Conwell wrote a biography of Wanamaker.

In the reference to "his yoke fellow" at the close of his "Appreciation" statement, we understand it to represent that the hard work, inexhaustible energy, tears, sweat, dedication, convictions, industry, creative genius, and achievements in Wanamaker's life were in close parallel and strong alignment with Conwell's lifework. Much of what they believed in and shared in common, was the love they felt for people.

The editor hopes that this interpretation helps the reader to understand what Wanamaker meant by this expression, "His yoke fellow."

PREFACE

Friends.—This lecture has been delivered under these circumstances: I visit a town or city, and try to arrive there early enough to see the postmaster, the barber, the keeper of the hotel, the principal of the schools, and the ministers of some of the churches. Then I go into some of the factories and stores, and talk with the people, and get into sympathy with the local conditions of that town or city and see what has been their history, what opportunities they had, and what they had failed to do—and every town fails to do something.

Then I go to the lecture and talk to those people about the subjects which apply to their locality. "Acres of Diamonds"—the idea—has continuously been precisely the same. The idea is that in this country of ours every person has the opportunity to make more of himself than he does in his own environment, with his own skill, with his own energy, and with his own friends.

Russell H. Conwell

Acres of Diamonds

WHEN going down the Tigris and Euphrates Rivers toward the ruins of Nineveh many years ago with a
party of English travelers, I found myself under the direction of an old Arab guide whom we hired up at Bagdad,
and I have often thought how that guide resembled our
barbers in certain mental characteristics. He thought that
it was not only his duty to guide us down those rivers, and
do what he was paid for doing, but also to entertain us
with stories curious and weird, ancient and modern, strange
and familiar. Many of them I have forgotten, and I am
glad I have, but there is one I shall never forget.

The old guide was leading my camel by its halter along
the banks of those ancient rivers, and he told me story after
story until I grew weary of his storytelling and ceased to
listen. I was irritated with that guide when he lost his
temper as I ceased listening. But I remember that he took
off his Turkish cap and swung it in a circle to get my
attention. I could see it through the corner of my eye, but I
determined not to look straight at him, for fear he would

This is the most recent and complete form of the lecture. It
happened to be delivered in Philadelphia, Dr. Conwell's home
city. When he says "right here in Philadelphia," he means the
home city, town, or village of every reader of this book, just as he
would use the name of it if delivering the lecture there, instead
of doing it through the pages which follow.

tell another story. I did finally look, and as soon as I did, he went right into another story.

Said he: "I will tell you a story now which I reserve for my particular friends." When he emphasized the words "particular friends," I listened, and I have ever been glad I did. I really feel devoutly thankful, that there are 1,674 young men who have been carried through college by this lecture who are also glad that I did listen.

The old guide told me that there once lived not far from the River Indus an ancient Persian by the name of Ali Hafed. He said that Ali Hafed owned a very large farm, that he had orchards, grain fields, and gardens; that he had money at interest, and was a wealthy and contented man. He was contented because he was wealthy, and wealthy because he was contented. One day there visited that old Persian farmer one of those ancient Buddhist priests, one of the wise men of the East. He sat down by the fire and told the old farmer how this world of ours was made. He said that this world was once a mere bank of fog, and that the Almighty thrust His finger into this bank of fog, and began slowly to move His finger around, increasing the speed until at last He whirled this bank of fog into a solid ball of fire. Then it went rolling through the universe, burning its way through other banks of fog, and condensed the moisture without, until it fell in floods of rain upon its hot surface, and cooled the outward crust. Then the internal fires bursting outward through the crust threw up the mountains and hills, the valleys, the plains and prairies of this wonderful world of ours. If this internal molten mass came bursting out and cooled very quickly it became granite; less quickly, copper, less quickly, silver, less quickly, gold, and, after gold, diamonds were made.

Said the old priest, "A diamond is a congealed drop of sunlight." Now that is literally, scientifically true, that a diamond is an actual deposit of carbon from the sun. The old priest told Ali Hafed that if he had one diamond the size of his thumb he could purchase the county, and if he had a mine of diamonds he could place his children upon thrones through the influence of their great wealth.

Ali Hafed heard all about diamonds, how much they were worth, and went to his bed that night poor man. He had not lost anything, but he was poor because he was discontented, and discontented because he feared he was poor. He said, "I want a mine of diamonds," and he lay awake all night.

Early in the morning he sought out the priest. I know by experience that a priest is very cross when awakened early in the morning, and when he shook that old priest out of his dreams, Ali Hafed said to him:

"Will you tell me where I can find diamonds?"

"Diamonds! What do you want with diamonds?"

"Why, I wish to be immensely rich."

"Well, then, go along and find them. That is all you have to do; go and find them, and then you have them."

"But I don't know where to go."

"Well, if you will find a river that runs through white sands, between high mountains, in those white sands you will always find diamonds."

"I don't believe there is any such river."

"Oh yes, there are plenty of them. All you have to do is to go and find them, and then you have them."

Said Ali Hafed, "I will go."

So he sold his farm, collected his money, left his family in charge of a neighbor, and away he went in search of diamonds. He began his search, very properly to my mind, at the Mountains of the Moon. Afterward, he came around into Palestine, then wandered on into Europe, and at last when his money was all spent and he was in rags, wretchedness, and poverty, he stood on the shore of that bay at

Barcelona, in Spain, when a great tidal wave came rolling in between the pillars of Hercules, and the poor, afflicted, suffering, dying man could not resist the awful temptation to cast himself into that incoming tide, and he sank beneath its foaming crest, never to rise in this life again.

When that old guide had told me that awfully sad story, he stopped the camel I was riding on and went back to fix the baggage that was coming off another camel, and I had an opportunity to muse over his story while he was gone. I remember saying to myself, "Why did he reserve that story for his 'particular friends'?" There seemed to be no beginning, no middle, no end, nothing to it. That was the first story I had ever heard told in my life, and would be the first one I ever read, in which the hero was killed in the first chapter. I had but one chapter of that story, and the hero was dead.

When the guide came back and took up the halter of my camel, he went right ahead with the story, into the second chapter, just as though there had been no break.

The man who purchased Ali Hafed's farm one day led his camel into the garden to drink, and as that camel put its nose into the shallow water of that garden brook, Ali Hafed's successor noticed a curious flash of light from the white sands of the stream. He pulled out a black stone having an eye of light reflecting all the hues of the rainbow. He took the pebble into the house and put it on the mantle which covers the central fires, and forgot all about it.

A few days later this same old priest came in to visit Ali Hafed's successor, and the moment he opened that drawing room door he saw that flash of light on the mantel, and he rushed up to it, and shouted: "Here is a diamond! Has Ali Hafed returned?"

"Oh no, Ali Hafed has not returned, and that is not a diamond. That is nothing but a stone we found right out here in our own garden."

"But," said the priest, "I tell you I know a diamond when I see it. I know positively that is a diamond."

Then together they rushed out into that old garden and stirred up the white sands with their fingers, and lo! there came up other more beautiful and valuable gems than the first. "Thus," said the guide to me, and, friends, it is historically true, "was discovered the diamond mine of Golconda, the most magnificent diamond mine in all the history of mankind, excelling the Kimberly itself. The Kohinoor, and the Orloff of the crown jewels of England and Russia, the largest on earth, came from that mine."

When that old Arab guide told me the second chapter of his story, he then took off his Turkish cap and swung it around in the air again to get my attention to the moral. Those Arab guides have morals to their stories, although they are not always moral. As he swung his hat, he said to me, "Had Ali Hafed remained at home and dug in his own cellar, or underneath his own wheat fields, or in his own garden, instead of wretchedness, starvation, and death by suicide in a strange land, he would have had 'acres of diamonds.' For every acre of that old farm, yes, every shovelful, afterward revealed gems which since have decorated the crowns of monarchs.

When he had added the moral to his story I saw why he reserved it for his "particular friends." But I did not tell him I could see it. It was that mean old Arab's way of going around a thing like a lawyer, to say indirectly what he did not dare say directly, that in his private opinion there was a certain young man then traveling down the Tigris River that might better be at home in America. I did not tell him I could see that, but I told him his story reminded me of one, and told it to him quickly and I think I will tell it to you.

I told him of a man out in California in 1847, who owned a ranch. He heard they had discovered gold in southern California, and so with a passion for gold he sold his ranch to Colonel Sutter, and away he went, never to come back. Colonel Sutter put a mill upon a stream that ran through that ranch, and one day his little girl brought some wet sand from the raceway into their home and sifted it through her fingers before the fire, and in that falling sand a visitor saw the first shining scales of real gold that were ever discovered in California. The man who had owned that ranch wanted gold, and he could have secured it for the mere taking. Indeed, thirty-eight millions of dollars has been taken out of a very few acres since then. About eight years ago I delivered this lecture in a city that stands on that farm, and they told me that a one-third owner for years and years had been getting one hundred and twenty dollars in gold every fifteen minutes, sleeping or waking, without taxation. You and I would enjoy an income like that—if we didn't have to pay an income tax.

But a better illustration than that really occurred here in our own Pennsylvania. If there is anything I enjoy above another on the platform, it is to get one of these German audiences in Pennsylvania before me, and fire that at them, and I enjoy it tonight. There was a man living in Pennsylvania, not unlike some Pennsylvanians you have seen, who owned a farm, and he did with that farm just what I should do with a farm if I owned one in Pennsylvania—he sold it. But before he sold it he decided to secure employment collecting coal oil for his cousin, who was in the business in Canada, where they first discovered oil on this continent. They dipped it from the running streams at that early time. So this Pennsylvania farmer wrote to his cousin asking for employment. You see, friends, this farmer was not altogether a foolish man. No, he was not. He did not leave his farm until he had something else to do. *Of all the simpletons the stars shine on I don't know of a worse one than the man who leaves one job before he has gotten another.* That has especial reference to my profession and has no reference whatever to a man seeking a divorce. When he wrote to his cousin for employment, his cousin replied, "I cannot engage you because you know nothing about the oil business."

Well, then the old farmer said, "I will know," and with most commendable zeal (characteristic of the students of Temple University) he set himself at the study of the whole subject. He began away back at the second day of God's creation when this world was covered thick and deep with that rich vegetation which since has turned into the primitive beds of coal. He studied the subject until he found that the drainings of those rich beds of coal furnished the coal oil that was worth pumping, and then he found how it came up with the living springs. He studied until he knew what it looked like, smelled like, tasted like, and how to refine it. Now said he in his letter to his cousin, "I understand the oil business." His cousin answered, "All right, come on."

So he sold his farm, according to the county record, for $833 (even money, "no cents"). He had scarcely gone from that place before the man who purchased the spot went out to arrange for the watering of the cattle. He found the previous owner had gone out years before and put a plank across the brook back of the barn, edgewise into the surface of the water just a few inches. The purpose of that plank at that sharp angle across the brook was to throw over to the other side a dreadful-looking scum through which the cattle would not put their noses. But with the plank there to throw it all over to one side, the cattle would drink below, and thus that man who had gone to Canada had been himself damming back for twenty-three years a flood of coal oil which the state geologists of Pennsylvania declared to us ten years later was even then worth a hundred millions of dollars to our state, and four years ago our geologist declared the discovery to be worth to our state a thousand millions of dollars. The man who owned that territory on which the city of Titusville now stands, and those Pleasantville valleys, had studied the subject from the second day of God's creation clear down to the present time. He studied it until he knew all about it, and yet he is said to have sold the whole of it for $833 and again I say, "no sense."

But I need another illustration. I found it in Massachusetts, and I am sorry I did because that is the state I came from. This young man in Massachusetts furnishes just another phase of my thought. He went to Yale College and studied mines and mining, and became such an adept as a mining engineer that he was employed by the authorities of the university to train students who were behind their classes. During his senior year he earned $15 a week for doing that work. When he graduated they raised his pay from $15 to $45 a week, and offered him a professorship, and as soon as they did he went right home to his mother.

If they had raised that boy's pay from $15 to $15.60 he would have stayed and been proud of the place, but when they put it up to $45 at one leap, he said, "Mother, I won't work for $45 a week. The idea of a man with a brain like mine working for $45 a week! Let's go out to California and stake out gold mines and silver mines, and be immensely rich."

Said his mother, "Now, Charlie, it is just as well to be happy as it is to be rich."

"Yes," said Charlie, "but it is just as well to be rich and happy, too." And they were both right about it. As he was an only son and she a widow, of course he had his way. They always do.

They sold out in Massachusetts, and instead of going to California they went to Wisconsin where he went into the employ of the Superior Copper Mining Company at $15 a week again, but with the proviso in his contract that he should have an interest in any mines he should discover for the company. I don't believe he ever discovered a mine, and if I am looking in the face of any stockholder of that copper company you wish he had discovered something or other. I have friends who are not here because they could not afford a ticket, who did have stock in that company at the time this young man was employed there. This young man went out there, and I have not heard a word from him. I don't know what became of him, and I don't know whether he found any mines or not, but I don't believe he ever did.

But I do know the other end of the line. He had scarcely gotten out of the old homestead before the succeeding owner went out to dig potatoes. The potatoes were already growing in the ground when he bought the farm, and as the old farmer was bringing in a basket of potatoes it hugged very tight between the ends of the stone fence. You know in Massachusetts our farms are nearly all stone wall. There you are obliged to be very economical of front gateways in order to have some place to put the stone. When that basket hugged so tight he set it down on the ground, and then dragged on one side, and pulled on the other side, and as he was dragging that basket through, this farmer noticed in the upper and outer corner of that stone wall, right next the gate, a block of native silver eight inches square. That professor of mines, mining, and mineralogy who knew so much about the subject that he would not work for $45 a week, when he sold that homestead in Massachusetts sat right on that silver to make the bargain. He was born on that homestead, was brought up there, and had gone back and forth rubbing the stone with his sleeve until it reflected his countenance, and seemed to say, "Here is a hundred thousand dollars right down here just for the taking." But he would not take it. It was in a home in Newburyport, Massachusetts, and there was no silver there, all away off—well, I don't know where, and he did not, but somewhere else, and he was a professor of mineralogy.

My friends, that mistake is very universally made, and why should we even smile at him? I often wonder what has become of him. I do not know at all, but I will tell you what I guess as a Yankee. I guess that he sits out there by his fireside tonight with his friends gathered around him, and he is saying to them something like this: "Do you know that man Conwell who lives in Philadelphia?"

"Oh yes, I have heard of him."

"Do you know that man Jones that lives in Philadelphia?"

"Yes, I have heard of him, too."

Then he begins to laugh, and shakes his sides, and says to his friends, "Well, they have done just the same thing I did, precisely"—and that spoils the whole joke, for you and I have done the same thing he did, and while we sit here and laugh at him he has a better right to sit out there and laugh at us. I know I have made the same mistakes, but, of course, that does not make any difference, because we don't expect the same man to preach and practise, too.

As I come here tonight and look around this audience, I am seeing again what through these fifty years I have continually seen—those who are making precisely that same mistake. I often wish I could see the younger people, and would that the Academy had been filled tonight with our high school scholars and our grammar school scholars, that I could have them to talk to. While I would have preferred such an audience as that, because they are most susceptible, as they have not grown up into their prejudices as we have, they have not gotten into any custom that they cannot break, they have not met with any failures as we have; and while I could perhaps do such an audience as that more good than I can do grown-up people, yet I will do the best I can with the material I have. I say to you that you have "acres of diamonds" in Philadelphia right where you now live. "Oh," but you will say, "you cannot know much about your city if you think there are any 'acres of diamonds' here."

I was greatly interested in that account in the newspaper of the young man who found that diamond in North Carolina. It was one of the purest diamonds that has ever been discovered, and it has several predecessors near the same locality. I went to a distinguished professor in mineralogy and asked him where he thought those diamonds came from. The professor secured the map of the geologic formations of our continent, and traced it. He said it went either through the underlying carboniferous strata adapted for such production, westward through Ohio and the Mississippi, or in more probability came eastward through Virginia and up the shore of the Atlantic Ocean. It is a fact that the diamonds were there, for they have been discovered and sold, and that they were carried down there during the drift period from some northern locality. Now who can say but some person going down with his drill in Philadelphia will find some trace of a diamond mine yet down here? Oh, friends! you cannot say that you are not over one of the greatest diamond mines in the world, for such a diamond as that only comes from the most profitable mines that are found on earth.

But it serves simply to illustrate my thought, which I emphasize by saying if you do not have the actual diamond mines literally, you have all that they would be good for to you. Now that the Queen of England has given the greatest compliment ever conferred upon American women for her attire because she appeared with no jewels at all at the late reception in England, it has almost done away with the use of diamonds anyhow. All you would care for would be the few you would wear if you wish to be modest, and the rest you would sell for money.

Now then, I say again that the opportunity to get rich, to attain unto great wealth, is here in Philadelphia now, within the reach of almost every man and woman who hears me speak tonight, and I mean just what I say. I have not come to this platform even under these circumstances to recite something to you. I have come to tell you what in God's sight I believe to be the truth, and if the years of life have been of any value to me in the attainment of common sense, I know I am right—that the men and women sitting here, who found it difficult perhaps to buy a ticket to this lecture or gathering tonight, have within their reach "acres of diamonds," opportunities to get largely wealthy. There never was a place on earth more adapted than the city of Philadelphia today, and never in the history of the world did a poor person without capital have such an opportunity to get rich quickly and honestly as he has now in our city. I say it is the truth, and I want you to accept it as such, for if you think I have come to simply recite something, then I would better not be here. I have no time to waste in any such talk, but to say the things I believe, and unless some of you get richer for what I am saying tonight, my time is wasted.

I say that you ought to get rich and it is your duty to get rich. How many of my pious brethren say to me, "Do you, a Christian minister, spend your time going up and down the country advising young people to get rich, to get money?"

"Yes, of course I do."

They say, "Isn't that awful! Why don't you preach the gospel instead of preaching about man's making money?"

"Because to make money honestly is to preach the gospel. That is the reason. The men who get rich may be the most honest men you find in the community."

"Oh, but" says some young man here tonight, "I have been told all my life that if a person has money he is very dishonest and dishonorable and mean and contemptible."

My friend, that is the reason why you have none, because you have that idea of people. The foundation of your faith is altogether false. Let me say here clearly, and say it briefly, though subject to discussion which I have not time for here, ninety-eight out of one hundred of the rich men of America are honest. That is why they are rich. That is why they are trusted with money. That is why they carry on great enterprises and find plenty of people to work with them. It is because they are honest men.

Says another young man, "I hear sometimes that some men get millions of dollars dishonestly." Yes, of course you do, and so do I. But they are so rare a thing in fact that the newspapers talk about them all the time as a matter of news until you get the idea that all the other rich men got rich dishonestly.

My friend, you take and drive me—if you furnish the auto—out into the suburbs of Philadelphia, and introduce me to the people who own their homes around this great city, those beautiful homes with gardens and flowers, those

magnificent homes, so lovely in their art, and I will introduce you to the very best people in character as well as in
enterprise in our city, and you know I will. A man is not
really a true man until he owns his own home, and they
that own their homes are made more honorable and honest
and pure and true and economical and careful, by owning
the home.

For a person to have money, even in large sums, is
not an inconsistent thing. We preach against covetousness.
You know we do, in the pulpit, and oftentimes preach
against it so long and use the terms about "filthy lucre" so
extremely that Christians get the idea that when we stand
in the pulpit we believe it is wicked for any man to have
money—until the collection-basket goes around, and then
we almost swear at the people because they don't give
more money. Oh, the inconsistency of such doctrines as
that!

**Money is power, and you ought to be reasonably
ambitious to have it.** You ought because you can do more
good with it than you could without it. Money printed
your Bible, money builds your churches, money sends your
missionaries, and money pays your preachers, and you
would not have many of them, either, if you did not pay
them. I am always willing that my church should raise my
salary, because the church that pays the largest salary always raises it the easiest. You never knew an exception to
it in your life. The man who gets the largest salary can do
the most good with the power that is furnished to him. Of
course, he can if his spirit be right to use it for what it is
given to him.

I say, then, you ought to have money. If you can
honestly attain unto riches in Philadelphia, it is your Christian and godly duty to do so. It is a great mistake of these

pious people to think you must be awfully poor in order to be pious.

Some men say, "Don't you sympathize with the poor people?" Of course I do, or else I would not have been lecturing these years. I won't give in but what I sympathize with the poor, but the number of poor who are to be sympathized with is very small. To sympathize with a man whom God has punished for his sins, thus to help him when God would still continue a just punishment, is to do wrong, no doubt about it, and we do that more than we help those who are deserving. While we should sympathize with God's poor—that is, those who cannot help themselves—let us remember there is not a poor person in the United States who was not made poor by his own shortcomings, or by the shortcomings of someone else. It is all wrong to be poor anyhow. Let us give in to that argument and pass that to one side.

A gentleman gets up back there, and says, "Don't you think there are some things in this world that are better than money?" Of course I do, but I am talking about money now. Of course there are some things higher than money. Oh, yes, I know by the grave that has left me standing alone that there are some things in this world that are higher and sweeter and purer than money. Well do I know there are some things higher and grander than gold. Love is the grandest thing on God's earth, but fortunate the lover who has plenty of money. **Money is power, money is force, money will do good as well as harm. In the hands of good men and women it can accomplish, and has accomplished, good.**

I hate to leave that behind me. I heard a man get up in a prayer meeting in our city and thank the Lord he was "one of God's poor." Well, I wonder what his wife thinks about that? She earns all the money that comes into that house, and he smokes a part of that on the veranda. I don't want to see any more of the Lord's poor of that kind, and I don't believe the Lord does. And yet there are some people who think in order to be pious you must be awfully poor and awfully dirty. That does not follow at all. While we sympathize with the poor, let us not teach a doctrine like that.

Yet the age is prejudiced against advising a Christian man (or, as a Jew would say, a godly man) from attaining unto wealth. The prejudice is so universal and the years are far enough back, I think, for me to safely mention that years ago up at Temple University there was a young man in our theological school who thought he was the only pious student in that department. He came into my office one evening and sat down by my desk, and said to me: "Mr. President, I think it is my duty, sir, to come in and labor with you."

"What has happened now?"

Said he, "I heard you say at the Academy, at the Peirce School commencement, that you thought it was an honorable ambition for a young man to desire to have wealth, and that you thought it made him temperate, made him anxious to have a good name, and made him industrious. You spoke about man's ambition to have money helping to make him a good man. Sir, I have come to tell you the Holy Bible says that "money is the root of all evil."

I told him I had never seen it in the Bible, and advised him to go out into the chapel and get the Bible, and show me the place. So out he went for the Bible, and soon he stalked into my office with the Bible open, with all the bigoted pride of the narrow sectarian, or of one who founds his Christianity on some misinterpretation of Scripture. He flung the Bible down on my desk, and fairly squealed into my ear: "There it is, Mr. President; you can read it for yourself."

I said to him: "Well, young man, you will learn when you get a little older that you cannot trust another denomination to read the Bible for you. You belong to another denomination. You are taught in theological school, however, that emphasis is exegesis. Now, will you take that Bible and read it yourself, and give the proper emphasis to it?"

He took the Bible, and proudly read, "'The love of money is the root of all evil.'"

Then he had it right, and when one does quote aright from that same old Book he quotes the absolute truth. I have lived through fifty years of the mightiest battle that old Book has ever fought, and I have lived to see its banners flying free, for never in the history of this world did the great minds of earth so universally agree that the Bible is true—all true—as they do at this very hour.

So I say that when he quoted right, of course he quoted the absolute truth. "The love of money is the root of all evil." He who tries to attain unto it too quickly, or dishonestly, will fall into many snares, no doubt about that. The love of money. What is that? It is making an idol of money, and idolatry pure and simple everywhere is condemned by the Holy Scriptures and by man's common sense. The man that worships the dollar instead of thinking of the purposes for which it ought to be used, the man who simply idolizes money, the miser that hoards his money in the cellar, or hides it in his stocking, or refuses to invest it where it will do the world good, that man who hugs the dollar until the eagle squeals, has in him the root of all evil.

I think I will leave that behind me now and answer the question of nearly all of you who are asking, "Is there opportunity to get rich in Philadelphia?"

Well, now, how simple a thing it is to see where it is, and the instant you see where it is, it is yours. Some old gentleman gets up back there and says, "Mr. Conwell, have you lived in Philadelphia for thirty-one years and don't know that the time has gone by when you can make anything in this city?"

"No, I don't think it is."

"Yes, it is; I have tried it."

"What business are you in?"

" I kept a store here for twenty years, and never made over a thousand dollars in the whole twenty years."

"Well, then, you can measure the good you have been to this city by what this city has paid you, because a man can judge very well what he is worth by what he receives; that is, in what he is to the world at this time. If you have not made over a thousand dollars in twenty years in Philadelphia, it would have been better for Philadelphia if they had kicked you out of the city nineteen years and nine months ago. A man has no right to keep a store in Philadelphia twenty years and not make at least five hundred thousand dollars, even though it be a corner grocery uptown." You say you cannot make five thousand dollars in a store now. Oh, my friends, if you will just take only four blocks around you, and find out what the people want and what you ought to supply and set them down with your pencil and figure up the profits you would make if you did supply them, you would very soon see it. There is wealth right within the sound of your voice.

Someone says: "You don't know anything about business. A preacher never knows a thing about business." Well, then, I will have to prove that I am an expert. I don't like to do this, but I have to do it because my testimony will not be taken if I am not an expert. My father kept a country store, and if there is any place under the stars where a man gets all sorts of experience in every kind of mercantile transaction, it is in the country store. I am not proud of my experience, but sometimes when my father was away he would leave me in charge of the store, though fortunately for him that was not very often. But this did occur many times, friends: A man would come in the store, and say to me, "Do you keep jackknives?"

"No, we don't keep jackknives," and I went off whistling a tune. What did I care about that man, anyhow?

Then another farmer would come in and ask, "Do you keep jackknives?"

"No, we don't keep jackknives." Then I went away and whistled another tune.

Then a third man came right in the same door and asked, "Do you keep jackknives?"

"No. Why is every one around here asking for jackknives? Do you suppose we are keeping this store to supply the whole neighborhood with jackknives?"

Do you carry on your store like that in Philadelphia? The difficulty was I had not then learned that **the foundation of godliness and the foundation principle of success in business are both the same, precisely.**

The man who says, "I cannot carry my religion into business" advertises himself either as being an imbecile in business, or on the road to bankruptcy, or a thief—one of the three, sure. He will fail within a very few years. He certainly will if he doesn't carry his religion into business. If I had been carrying on my father's store on a Christian plan, godly plan, I would have had a jackknife for the third man when he called for it. Then I would have actually done him a kindness, and I would have received a reward myself, which it would have been my duty to take.

There are some over-pious Christian people who think if you take any profit on anything you sell that you are an unrighteous man. On the contrary, you would be a criminal to sell goods for less than they cost. You have no right to do that. You cannot trust a man with your money who cannot take care of his own. You cannot trust a man in your family that is not true to his own wife. You cannot trust a man in the world who does not begin with his own heart, his own character and his own life.

It would have been my duty to have furnished a jack-knife to the third man, or the second, and to have sold it to him and actually profited myself. I have no more right to sell goods without making a profit on them than I have to overcharge him dishonestly beyond what they are worth. But I should so sell each bill of goods that the person to whom I sell shall make as much as I make.

To live and let live is the principle of the gospel, and the principle of everyday common sense. Oh young person, hear me—live as you go along. Do not wait until you have reached my years before you begin to enjoy anything of this life. If I had the millions back, or fifty cents of it, which I have tried to earn in these years, it would not do me anything like the good that it does me now in this almost sacred presence tonight. Oh, yes, I am paid over and over a hundredfold tonight for dividing as I have tried to do in some measure as I went along through the years. I ought not speak that way, it sounds egotistic, but I am old enough now to be excused for that. **I should have helped my fellow men, which I have tried to do, and everyone should try to do, and get the happiness of it.** The man who goes home with the sense that he has stolen a dollar that day, that he has robbed a man of what was his honest due, is not going to sweet rest. He arises tired in the morning, and goes with an unclean conscience to his work the next day. He is not a successful man at all, although he may have laid up millions. But **the man who has gone through life dividing always with his fellowmen,** making and demanding his own rights and his own profits, and giving to every other man his rights and profits, **lives every day, and not only that, but it is the royal road to great wealth.** The history of the thousands of millionaires shows that to be the case.

The man over there who said he could not make anything in a store in Philadelphia has been carrying on his store on the wrong principle. Suppose I go into your store tomorrow morning and ask, "Do you know neighbor A, who lives one square away, at house No. 1240?"

"Oh, yes, I have met him. He deals here at the corner store."

"Where did he come from?"

"I don't know."

"How many does he have in his family?"

"I don't know."

"What ticket does he vote?"

"I don't know."

"What church does he go to?"

"I don't know, and don't care. What are you asking all these questions for?"

If you had a store in Philadelphia, would you answer me like that? If so, then you are conducting your business just as I carried on my father's business in Worthington, Massachusetts. You don't know where your neighbor came from when he moved to Philadelphia, and you don't care. *If you had cared you would be a rich man now.* If you had cared enough about him to take an interest in his affairs, to find out what he needed, you would have been rich. But you go through the world saying, "No opportunity to get rich," and there is the fault right at your own door.

But another young man gets up over there and says, "I cannot take up the mercantile business." (While I am talking of trade it applies to every occupation.)

"Why can't you go into the mercantile business?"

"Because I haven't any capital."

Oh, the weak and dudish creature that can't see over its collar! It makes a person weak to see these little dudes standing around the corners and saying, "Oh, if I had plenty of capital, how rich I would get."

"Young man, do you think you are going to get rich on capital?"

"Certainly."

"Well," I say, "Certainly not." If your mother has plenty of money, and she will set you up in business, you will "set her up in business," supplying you with capital.

The moment a young man or woman gets more money than he or she has grown to by practical experience, that moment has gotten a curse. It is no help to a young man or woman to inherit money. It is no help to your children to leave them money, but if you leave them education, if you leave them a noble character, if you leave them a wide circle of friends, if you leave them an honorable name, it is far better than that they should have money. It would be worse for them, worse for the nation, that they should have any money at all. Oh, young man or woman, if you have inherited money, don't regard it as a help. It will curse you through your years, and deprive you of the very best things of human life. There is no class of people to be pitied so much as the inexperienced sons and daughters of the rich of our generation. I pity the rich man's son. He can never know the best things in life.

One of the best things in our life is when a young man has earned his own living, and when he becomes engaged to a lovely young woman, and makes up his mind to have a home of his own. Then, with that same love comes also that divine inspiration toward better things, and he begins to save his money. He begins to leave off his bad habits and put money in the bank. When he has a few hundred dollars he goes out in the suburbs to look for a home. He goes to the savings bank, perhaps, for half of the value, and then goes for his wife, and when he takes his bride over the threshold of that door for the first time he says in words of eloquence my voice can never touch: "I have earned this home myself. It is all mine, and I divide with thee." That is the grandest moment a human heart may ever know.

But a rich man's son can never know that. He takes his bride into a finer mansion, it may be, but he is obliged to go all the way through and say to his wife, " My mother gave me that, my mother gave me that, and my mother gave me this," until his wife wishes she had married his mother. I pity the rich man's son.

The statistics of Massachusetts show that not one rich man's son out of seventeen ever dies rich.

I pity the rich man's sons unless they have the good sense of the elder Vanderbilt, which sometimes happens. He went to his father and said, "Did you earn all your money?"

"I did, my son. I began to work on a ferry-boat for twenty-five cents a day."

"Then," said his son, "I will have none of your money," and he too, tried to get employment on a ferry-boat that Saturday night. He could not get one there, but he did get a place for three dollars a week. Of course, if a rich man's son will do that, he will get the discipline of a poor boy that is worth more than a university education to any man. He would then be able to take care of the millions of his father. But as a rule the rich men will not let their sons do the very thing that made them great. As a rule, the rich man will not allow his son to work. And his mother! Why, she would think it was a social disgrace if her poor, weak, little lily-fingered, sissy sort of a boy had to earn his living with honest toil. I have no pity for such rich men's sons.

At a banquet here in Philadelphia there sat beside me a kind-hearted young man, who said, "Mr. Conwell, you have been sick for two or three years. When you go out, take my limousine, and it will take you up to your house on Broad Street."

I thanked him very much. I got on to the seat with the driver of that limousine, outside, and when we were going up I asked the driver, "How much did this limousine cost?"

"Six thousand eight hundred, and he had to pay the duty on it."

"Well," I asked, "does the owner of this machine ever drive it himself?"

At that, the chauffeur laughed so heartily that he lost control of his machine. He was so surprised at the question that he ran up on the sidewalk, and around a corner lamp post out into the street again. And when he got out into the street he laughed till the whole machine trembled.

He said: "He drive this machine! Oh, he would be lucky if he knew enough to get out when we get there."

I must tell you about a rich man's son at Niagara Falls. I came in from the lecture to the hotel, and as I approached the desk of the clerk there stood a millionaire's son from New York. He was an indescribable specimen of anthropologic potency. He had a skullcap on one side of his head, with a gold tassel on the top of it, and a gold-headed cane under his arm with more in it than in his head. It is a very difficult thing to describe that young man. He wore an eyeglass that he could not see through, patent-leather boots that he could not walk in, and pants that he could not sit down in—dressed like a grasshopper.

This human cricket came up to the clerk's desk just as I entered, adjusted his unseeing eye-glass, and spake in this wise to the clerk. You see, he thought it was "Hinglish, you know," to lisp. "Thir, will you have the kindness to supply me with thome papah and enwelophs!" The hotel clerk measured that man quick, and he pulled the envelopes and paper out of a drawer, threw them across the counter toward the young man, and then turned away to his books. You should have seen that young man when those envelopes came across that counter. He swelled up like a gobbler turkey, adjusted his unseeing eye-glass, and yelled: "Come right back here. Now thir, will you order a thervant to take that papah and enwelophs to yondah dethk."

Oh, the poor, miserable, contemptible American monkey! He could not carry paper and envelopes twenty feet. I suppose he could not get his arms down to do it. I have no pity for such travesties upon human nature. If you have not capital, young man, I am glad of it. What you need is common sense, not copper cents.

The best thing I can do is to illustrate by actual facts well-known to you all. A. T. Steward, a poor boy in New York, had $1.50 to begin life on. He lost 87 1/2 cents of that on the very first venture. How fortunate that young man who loses the first time he gambles. That boy said, "I will never gamble again in business," and he never did. How came he to lose 87 1/2 cents? You probably all know the story about he lost it—because he bought some needles, threads, and buttons to sell which people did not want, and had them left on his hands, a dead loss. Said the boy, "I will not lose any more money in that way."

Then he went around first to the doors and asked the people what they did want. Then when he had found out what they wanted he invested his 62 1/2 cents to supply a known demand.

Study it wherever you choose—in business, in your profession, in your housekeeping, whatever your life, **that one thing is the secret of success. You must first know the demand. You must first know what people need, and then invest yourself where you are most needed.** A. T. Stewart went on that principle until he was worth what amounted afterward to forty millions of dollars, owning the very store in which Mr. Wanamaker carries on his great work in New York. His fortune was made by his losing something, which taught him the great lesson that he must only invest himself or his money in something that people need. When will you salesmen learn it? When will you manufacturers learn that you must know the changing needs of humanity if you would succeed in life? Apply yourselves as manufacturers or merchants or workmen to supply that human need. It is a great principle as broad as humanity and as deep as the Scripture itself.

The best illustration I ever heard was of John Jacob Astor. You know that he made the money of the Astor family when he lived in New York. He came across the sea in debt for his fare. But that poor boy with nothing in his pocket made the fortune of the Astor family on one principle. Some young man here tonight will say, "Well, they could make those fortunes over in New York, but they could not do it in Philadelphia!"

My friends, did you ever read that wonderful book of Jacob Riis (his memory is sweet to us because of his recent death), wherein is given his statistical account of the records taken in 1889 of 107 millionaires of New York? If you read the account you will see that out of the 107 millionaires only seven made their money in New York. Out of the 107 millionaires worth ten million dollars in real estate then, 67 of them made their money in towns of less than 3,500 inhabitants. The richest man in this country today, if you read the real-estate values, has never moved away from a town of 3,500 inhabitants. It makes not so much difference *where* you are as *who* you are. But if you cannot get rich in Philadelphia you certainly cannot do it in New York.

Now, John Jacob Astor illustrated what can be done anywhere. He had a mortgage once on a millinery store, and they could not sell bonnets enough to pay the interest on his money. So he foreclosed that mortgage, took possession of the store, and went into partnership with the very same people, in the same store, with the same capital. He did not give them a dollar of capital. They had to sell goods to get any money. Then he left them alone in the store just as they had been before, and he went out and sat down on a bench in the park in the shade.

What was John Jacob Astor doing out there, and in partnership with people who had failed on his own hands? He had the most important and, to my mind, the most pleasant part of the partnership on his hands. For as John Jacob Astor sat on that bench he was watching the ladies as they went by; and where is the man who would not get rich at that business? As he sat on the bench if a lady passed him with her shoulders back and head up, and looked straight to the front, as if she did not care if all the world did gaze on her, then he studied her bonnet, and by the time it was out of sight he knew the shape of the frame, the color of the trimmings, and the crinklings in the feather. I sometimes try to describe a bonnet, but not always. I would not try to describe a modern bonnet. Where is the man that could describe one? This aggregation of all sorts of drift-wood stuck on the back of the head, or the side of the neck, like a rooster with only one tail feather left. But in John Jacob Astor's day there was some art about the millinery business, and he went to the millinery store and said to them: "Now put into the show window just such a bonnet as I describe to you, because I have already seen a lady who likes such a bonnet. Don't make up any more until I come back."

Then he went out and sat down again, and another lady passed him of a different form, of different complexion, with a different shape and color of bonnet. "Now," said he, "put such a bonnet as that in the show window."

He did not fill his show window uptown with a lot of hats and bonnets to drive people away, and then sit on the back stairs and bawl because people went to Wanamaker's to trade. He did not have a hat or a bonnet in that show window but what some lady liked before it was made up. The tide of custom began immediately to turn in, and that has been the foundation of the greatest store in New York in that line, and still exists as one of three stores. Its fortune was made by John Jacob Astor after they had failed in business, not by giving them any more money, but by finding out what the ladies liked for bonnets before they wasted any material in making them up. I tell you if a man could foresee the millinery business he could foresee anything under heaven!

Suppose I were to go through this audience tonight and ask you in this great manufacturing city if there are not opportunities to get rich in manufacturing. "Oh, yes," some young man says, "there are opportunities here still if you build with some trust and if you have two or three millions of dollars to begin with as capital."

Young man, the history of the breaking up of the trusts by that attack upon "big business" is only illustrating what is now the opportunity of the smaller man. The time never came in the history of the world when you could get rich so quickly manufacturing without capital as you can now.

But you will say, "You cannot do anything of the kind. You cannot start without capital." Young man, let me illustrate for a moment. I must do it. It is my duty to every young man and woman, because we are all going into business very soon on the same plan. Young man, remember if you know what people need, you have gotten more knowledge of a fortune than any amount of capital can give you.

There was a poor man out of work living in Hingham, Massachusetts. He lounged around the house until one day his wife told him to get out and work, and as he lived in Massachusetts, he obeyed his wife. He went out and sat down on the shore of the bay and whittled a soaked shingle into a wooden chain. His children that evening quarreled over it, and he whittled a second one to keep peace. While he was whittling the second one a neighbor came in and said: "Why don't you whittle toys and sell them? You could make money at that."

"Oh," he said, "I would not know what to make."

"Why don't you ask your own children right here in your own house what to make?"

"What is the use of trying that?" said the carpenter. "My children are different from other people's children." (I used to see people like that when I taught school.)

But he acted upon the hint, and the next morning when Mary came down the stairway, he asked, "What do you want for a toy?" She began to tell him she would like a doll's bed, a doll's washstand, a doll's carriage, a little doll's umbrella, and went on with a list of things that would take him a lifetime to supply. So, consulting his own children, in his own house, he took the firewood, for he had no money to buy lumber, and whittled those strong unpainted Hingham toys that were for so many years known all over the world. That man began to make those toys for his own children, and then made copies and sold them through the boot-and-shoe store next door. He began to make a little money, and a little more, and Mr. Lawson, in his *Frenzied Finance* says that man is the richest man in old Massachusetts, and I think it is the truth. And that man is worth a hundred millions of dollars today, and has been only thirty-four years making it on that one principle—that one must judge that what his own children like at home other people's children would like in their homes, too; to judge the human heart by oneself, by one's wife or by one's children. It is the royal road to success in manufacturing. "Oh," but you say, "didn't he have any capital?" Yes, a penknife, but I don't know that he had paid for that.

I spoke thus to an audience in New Britain, Connecticut, and a lady four seats back went home and tried to take off her collar, and the collar button stuck in the buttonhole. She threw it out and said, "I am going to get up something better than that to put on collars."

Her husband said: "After what Conwell said tonight, you see there is a need of an improved collar-fastener that is easier to handle. There is a human need; there is a great fortune. Now then, get up a collar-button and get rich."

He made fun of her, and consequently made fun of me, and that is one of the saddest things which comes over me like a deep cloud of midnight sometimes—although I have worked so hard for more than half a century, yet how little I have ever really done.

Notwithstanding the greatness and the handsomeness of your compliment tonight, I do not believe there is one in ten of you that is going to make a million of dollars because you are here tonight, but it is not my fault, it is yours. I say that sincerely. What is the use of my talking if people never do what I advise them to do?

When her husband ridiculed her, she made up her mind she would make a better collar-button, and when a woman makes up her mind "she will," and does not say anything about it, she does it. It was that New England woman who invented the snap button which you can find anywhere now. It was first a collar-button with a spring cap attached to the outer side. Any of you who wear modern waterproofs know the button that simply pushes together, and when you unbutton it you simply pull it apart. That is the button to which I refer, and which she invented. She afterward invented several other buttons, and then invested in more, and then was taken into partnership with great factories.

Now that woman goes over the sea every summer in her private steamship—yes, and takes her husband with her! If her husband were to die, she would have money enough left now to buy a foreign duke or count or some such title as that at the latest quotations.

Now what is my lesson in that incident? It is this: I told her then, though I did not know her, what I now say to you, "Your wealth is too near to you. You are looking right over it"; and she had to look over it because it was right under her chin.

I have read in the newspaper that a woman never invented anything. Well, that newspaper ought to begin again. Of course, I do not refer to gossip—I refer to machines and if I did I might better include the men. That newspaper could never appear if women had not invented something. Friends, think. Ye women, think! You say you cannot make a fortune because you are in some laundry, or running a sewing machine, it may be, or walking before some loom, and yet you can be a millionaire if you will but follow this almost infallible direction.

When you say a woman doesn't invent anything, I ask, Who invented the Jacquard loom that wove every stitch you wear? Mrs. Jacquard. The printer's roller was invented by a farmer's wife. Who invented the cotton gin of the South that enriched our country so amazingly? Mrs. General Greene invented the cotton gin and showed the idea to Mr. Whitney, and he like a man, seized it. Who was it that invented the sewing machine? If I would go to school tomorrow and ask your children they would say, "Elias Howe."

He was in the Civil War with me, and often in my tent. I heard him say that he worked fourteen years to get up that sewing machine. But his wife made up her mind one day that they would starve to death if there wasn't something or other invented pretty soon, and so in two hours she invented the sewing machine. Of course he took out the patent in his name. Men always do that. Who was it that invented the mower and the reaper? According to Mr. McCormick's confidential communication, so recently published, it was a West Virginia woman, who, after his father and he had failed altogether in making a reaper and gave it up, took a lot of shears and nailed them together on the edge of a board, with one shaft of each pair loose, and then wired them so that when she pulled the wire one way it closed them, and when she pulled the wire the other way it opened them, and there she had the principle of the mowing machine. If you look at a mowing machine, you will see it is nothing but a lot of shears. If a woman can invent a mowing machine, if a woman can invent a Jacquard loom, if a woman can invent a cotton gin, if a woman can invent a trolley switch—as she did and made the trolleys possible; if a woman can invent, as Mr. Carnegie said, the great iron squeezers that laid the foundation of all the steel millions of the United states, "we men" can invent anything under the stars.! I say that for the encouragement of the men.

Who are the great inventors of the world? Again this lesson comes before us. The great inventor sits next to you, or you are the person yourself. "Oh," but you will say, "I have never invented anything in my life." Neither did the great inventors until they discovered one great secret. Do you think it is a man with a head like a bushel measure or a man like a stroke of lightning? It is neither. The really great man is a plain, straightforward, everyday, common-sense man. You would not dream that he was a great inventor if you did not see something he had actually done. His neighbors do not regard him so great. You never see anything great over your back fence. You say there is no greatness among your neighbors. It is all away off somewhere else. Their greatness is ever so simple, so plain, so earnest, so practical, that the neighbors and friends never recognize it. True greatness is often unrecognized. That is sure. You do not know anything about the greatest men and women. I went out to write the life of General Garfield, and a neighbor, knowing I was in a hurry, and as there was a great crowd around the front door, took me around to General Garfield's back door and shouted, "Jim! Jim!" And very soon "Jim" came to the door and let me in, and I wrote the biography of one of the grandest men of the nation, and yet he was just the same old "Jim" to his neighbor. If you know a great man in Philadelphia and you should meet him tomorrow, you would say, "How are you, Sam?" or "Good morning, Jim." Of course you would. That is just what you would do.

One of my soldiers in the Civil War had been sentenced to death, and I went up to the White House in

Washington—sent there for the first time in my life—to see the President. I went into the waiting room and sat down with a lot of others on the benches, and the secretary asked one after another to tell him what they wanted. After the secretary had been through the line, he went in, and then came back to the door and motioned for me. I went up to that anteroom, and the secretary said: "That is the President's door right over there. Just rap on it and go right in." I never was so taken aback, friends, in all my life, never. The secretary himself made it worse for me, because he had told me how to go in and then went out another door to the left and shut that. There I was, in the hallway by myself before the president of the United States of America's door. I had been on fields of battle, where the shells did sometimes shriek and the bullets did sometimes hit me, but I always wanted to run. I have no sympathy with the old man who says, "I would just as soon march up to the cannon's mouth as eat my dinner." I have no faith in a man who doesn't know enough to be afraid when he is being shot at. I never was so afraid when the shells came around us at Antietam as I was when I went into that room that day; but I finally mustered the courage—I don't know how I ever did—and at arm's length tapped on the door. The man inside did not help me at all, but yelled out, "Come in and sit down!"

Well, I went in and sat down on the edge of a chair and wished I were in Europe, and the man at the table did not look up. He was one of the world's greatest men, and was made great by one single rule. Oh, that all the young people of Philadelphia were before me now and I could say just this one thing, and that they would remember it. I would give a lifetime for the effect it would have on our city and on civilization.

Abraham Lincoln's principle for greatness can be adopted by nearly all. This was his rule: **Whatsoever you have to do, put your whole mind into it and hold it there until all is done. That makes men great almost anywhere.** President Lincoln stuck to those papers at that table and did not look up at me, and I sat there trembling. Finally, when he had put the string around his papers, he pushed them over to one side and looked over to me, and a smile came over his worn face. He said: "I am a very busy man and have only a few minutes to spare. Now tell me in the fewest words what it is you want." I began to tell him, and mentioned the case, and he said: "I have heard all about it and you do not need to say any more. Mr. Stanton was talking to me only a few days ago about that. You can go to the hotel and rest assured that the President never did sign an order to shoot a boy under twenty years of age, and never will. You can say that to his mother."

Then he asked me, "How is it going in the field?"

I said, "We sometimes get discouraged."

And he said: "It is all right. We are going to win now. We are getting very near the light. No man ought to wish to be President of the United States, and I will be glad when I get through; then Tad and I are going out to Springfield, Illinois. I have bought a farm out there and I don't care if I again earn only twenty-five cents a day. Tad has a mule team, and we are going to plant onions."

Then he asked me, "Were you brought up on a farm?"

I said, "Yes; in the Berkshire Hills of Massachusetts." He then threw his leg over the corner of the big chair and said, "I have heard many a time, ever since I was young, that up there in those hills you have to sharpen the noses of the sheep in order to get down to the grass between the rocks." He was so familiar, so everyday, so farmer-like, that I felt right at home with him at once.

He then took hold of another roll of paper, and looked up at me and said, "Good morning." I took the hint then and got up and went out.

After I had gotten out I could not realize I had seen the President of the United States at all. But a few days later, when still in the city, I saw the crowd pass through the East Room by the coffin of Abraham Lincoln, and when I looked at the upturned face of the murdered President, I felt then that the man I had seen such a short time before, who, so simple a man, so plain a man, was one of the greatest men that God ever raised up to lead a nation on to ultimate liberty. Yet he was only "Old Abe" to his neighbors. When they had the second funeral, I was invited among others, and went out to see that same coffin put back in the tomb at Springfield. Around the tomb stood Lincoln's old neighbors, to whom he was just "Old Abe." Of course that is all they would say.

Did you ever see a man who struts around altogether too large to notice an ordinary working mechanic? Do you think he is great? He is nothing but a puffed-up balloon, held down by his big feet. There is no greatness there.

Who are the great men and women? My attention was called the other day to the history of a very little thing that made the fortune of a very poor man. It was an awful thing, and yet because of that experience he—not a great inventor or genius—invented the pin that now is called the safety pin, and out of that safety pin made the fortune of one of the great aristocratic families of this nation.

A poor man in Massachusetts who had worked in the nail works was injured at thirty-eight, and he could earn but little money. He was employed in the office to rub out the marks on the bills made by pencil memorandums, and he used a rubber until his hand grew tired. He then tied a piece of rubber on the end of a stick and worked it like a plane. His little girl came and said, "Why, you have a patent, haven't you?" The father said afterward, "My daughter told me when I took that stick and put the rubber on the end that there was a patent, and that was the first thought of that." He went to Boston and applied for his patent, and every one of you that has a rubber-tipped pencil in your pocket is now paying tribute to the millionaire. No capital, not a penny did he invest in it. All was income, all the way up into the millions.

But let me hasten to one other greater thought. "Show me the great men and women who live in Philadelphia." A gentleman over there will get up and say: "We don't have any great men in Philadelphia. They don't live here. They live away off in Rome or St. Petersburg or London or Manayunk, or anywhere else but here in our town." I have come now to the apex of my thought. I have come now to the heart of the whole matter and to the center of my struggle: Why isn't Philadelphia a greater city in its greater wealth? Why does New York excel Philadelphia? People say, "Because of her harbor." Why do so many other cities of the United States get ahead of Philadelphia now? There is only one answer, and that is because our own people talk down their own city. If there ever was a community on earth that has to be forced ahead, it is the city of Philadelphia. If we are to have a boulevard, talk it down; if we are going to have better schools, talk them down; if you wish to have wise legislation, talk it down; talk all the proposed improvements down. That is the only great wrong that I can lay at the feet of the magnificent Philadelphia that has been so universally kind to me. I say it is time we turn around in our city and begin to talk up the things that are in our city, and begin to set them before the world as the people of Chicago, New York, St. Louis, and San Francisco do. Oh, if we only could get that spirit out among our people, that we can do things in Philadelphia and do them well!

Arise, ye millions of Philadelphians, trust in God and man, and believe in the great opportunities that are right here—not over in New York or Boston, but here—for business, for everything that is worth living for on earth. There was never an opportunity greater. Let us talk up our own city.

But there are two other young men here tonight, and that is all I will venture to say, because it is too late. One over there gets up and says "There is going to be a great man in Philadelphia, but never was one."

"Oh, is that so? When are you going to be great?"

"When I am elected to some political office."

Young man, won't you learn a lesson in the primer of politics that it is a *prima facie* evidence of littleness to hold office under our form of government? Great men get into office sometimes, but what this country needs is men who will do what we tell them to do. This nation—where the people rule—is governed by the people, for the people, and so long as it is, then the officeholder is but the servant of the people. The Bible says the servant cannot be greater than the master. The Bible says, "He that is sent cannot be greater than He who sent Him." The people rule, or should rule, and if they do, we do not need the greater men in office. If the great men in America took our offices, we would change to an empire in the next ten years.

I know of a great many young women, now that woman's suffrage is coming, who say, "I am going to be President of the United States some day." I believe in woman's suffrage, and there is no doubt but what it is coming, and I am getting out of the way, anyhow. I may want an office by and by myself, but if the ambition for an office influences the women in their desire to vote, I want to say right here what I say to the young men, that if you only get the privilege of casting one vote, you don't get anything that is worthwhile. Unless you can control more than one vote, you will be unknown, and your influence so dissipated as practically not to be felt. This country is not run by votes. Do you think it is? It is governed by influence. It is governed by the ambitions and the enterprises which control votes. The young woman that thinks she is going to vote for the sake of holding an office is making an awful blunder.

That other young man gets up and says, "There are going to be great men in this country and in Philadelphia." "Is that so? When?" "When there comes a great war, when we get into difficulty through watchful waiting in Mexico; when we get into war with England over some frivolous deed, or with Japan or China or New Jersey or some distant country. Then I will march up to the cannon's mouth; I will sweep up among the glistening bayonets; I will leap into the arena and tear down the flag and bear it away in triumph. I will come home with stars on my shoulder, and hold every office in the gift of the nation, and I will be great." No, you won't. You think you are going to be made great by an office, but remember that if you are not great before you get the office, you won't be great when you secure it. It will only be a burlesque in that shape.

We had a Peace Jubilee here after the Spanish War. Out West they don't believe this, because they said, "Philadelphia would not have heard of any Spanish War until fifty years hence." Some of you saw the procession go up Broad Street. I was away, but the family wrote to me that the tally-ho coach with Lieutenant Hobson upon it stopped right at the front door and the people shouted, "Hurrah for Hobson!" If I had been there I would have yelled too, because he deserves much more of his country than he has ever received. But suppose I go into a school and ask, "Who sank the *Merrimac* at Santiago?" and if the pupils answer me, "Hobson," they will tell me seven-eighths of a lie. There were seven other heroes on that steamer, and they, by virtue of their position, were continually exposed to the Spanish fire, while Hobson, as an officer, might reasonably be behind the smokestack. You have gathered in this house your most intelligent people, and yet, perhaps, not one here can name the other seven men.

We ought not to so teach history. We ought to teach that, however humble a man's station may be, if he does his full duty in that place he is just as much entitled to the American people's honor as is the king upon his throne. But we do not so teach. We are now teaching everywhere that the generals do all the fighting.

I remember another illustration. I would leave it out but for the fact that when you go to the library to read this lecture, you will find this has been printed in it for twenty-five years. I shut my eyes—shut them close—and lo! I see the faces of my youth. Yes, they sometimes say to me, "Your hair is not white; you are working night and day without seeming ever to stop; you can't be old." But when I shut my eyes, like any other man of my years, oh, then come trooping back the faces of the loved and lost of long ago, and I know, whatever men may say, it is evening time.

I shut my eyes now and look back to my native town in Massachusetts, and I see the cattle showground on the mountain-top; I can see the horsesheds there. I can see the Congregational church; see the town hall and mountaineers' cottages; see a great assembly of people turning out, dressed resplendently, and I can see flags flying and handkerchiefs waving and hear bands playing. I can see that company of soldiers that had re-enlisted marching up on the cattle showground. I was but a boy, but I was captain of that company and puffed out with pride. A cambric needle would have burst me all to pieces. Then I thought it was the greatest event that ever came to man on earth. If you have ever thought you would like to be a king or queen, go and be received by the mayor.

The bands played, and all the people turned out to receive us. I marched up that Common so proud at the head of my troops, and we turned down into the town hall. They seated my soldiers down the center aisle and I sat down in the front seat. A great assembly of people—a hundred or two—came in to fill the town hall, so that they stood up all around. Then the town officers came in and formed a half circle. The mayor of the town sat in the middle of the platform. He was a man who had never held office before. He was a good man, but he thought an office made a man great. He came up and took his seat, adjusted his powerful spectacles, and looked around, when he suddenly spied me sitting there on a front seat. He came right forward on the platform and invited me up to sit with the town officers. No town officer ever took any notice of me before I went to war, except to advise the teacher to thrash me, and now I was invited up on the stand with the town officers. Oh my! The town mayor was then the emperor, the king of our day and our time. As I came up on the platform they gave me a chair about this far, I would say, from the front.

When I had seated myself, the chairman of the Selectmen arose and came forward to the table, and we all supposed he would introduce the Congregational minister, who was the only orator in town, and that he would give the oration to the returning soldiers. But, friends, you should have seen the surprise which ran over the audience when they discovered that the old fellow was going to deliver that speech himself. He had never made a speech in his life, but he fell into the same error that hundreds of other men have fallen into. It seems so strange that a man won't learn he must speak his piece as a boy if he intends to be an orator when he is grown, but he seems to think all he has to do is to hold an office to be a great orator.

So he came up to the front, and brought with him a speech which he had learned by heart walking up and down the pasture, where he had frightened the cattle. He brought the manuscript with him and spread it out on the table so as to be sure he might see it. He adjusted his spectacles and leaned over it for a moment and marched back on that platform, and then came forward like this— tramp, tramp, tramp. He must have studied the subject a great deal, when you come to think of it, because he assumed an "elocutionary" attitude. He rested heavily upon his left heel, threw back his shoulders, slightly advanced his right foot, opened the organs of speech, and advanced his right foot at an angle of forty-five. As he stood in that elocutionary attitude, friends, this is just the way that speech went. Some people say to me, "Don't you exaggerate?" That would be impossible. But I am here for the lesson and not for the story, and this is the way it went:

"Fellow citizens—" As soon as he heard his voice his fingers began to go like that, his knees began to shake, and then he trembled all over. He choked and swallowed and came around to the table to look at the manuscript. Then he gathered himself up with clenched fists and came back: "Fellow citizens, we are— Fellow citizens, we are—we are— we are—we are—we are—we are very happy—we are very happy—we are very happy. We are very happy to welcome back to their native town these soldiers who have fought and bled—and come back again to their native town. We are especially—we are especially—we are especially.

We are especially pleased to see with us today this young hero" (that meant me)—"this young hero who in imagination (friends, remember he said that; if he had not said "in imagination" I would not be egotistic enough to refer to it at all)—"this young hero who in imagination we have seen leading—we have seen leading—leading. We have seen leading his troops on to the deadly breach. We have seen his shining—we have seen his shining—we have seen his shining—his shining sword—flashing. Flashing in the sunlight, as he shouted to his troops, 'Come on'!"

Oh, dear, dear, dear! how little that good man knew about war. If he had known anything about war at all he ought to have known what any of my G. A. R. comrades here tonight will tell you is true, that it is next to a crime for an officer of infantry ever in time of danger to go ahead of his men. I, with my shining sword flashing in the sunlight, shouting to my troops, "Come on"! I never did it. Do you suppose I would get in front of my men to be shot in front by the enemy and in the back by my own men? That is no place for an officer. The place for the officer in actual battle is behind the line. How often, as a staff officer, I rode down the line, when our men were suddenly called to the line of battle, and the Rebel yells were coming out of the woods, and shouted: "Officers to the rear! Officers to the rear!" Then every officer gets behind the line of private soldiers and the higher the officer's rank the farther behind he goes. Not because he is any the less brave, but because the laws of war require that. And yet he shouted, "He with his shining sword—!" In that house there sat the company of my soldiers who had carried that boy across the Carolina rivers that he might not wet his feet. Some of them had gone far out to get a pig or a chicken. Some of them had gone to death under the shell-swept pines in the mountains of Tennessee, yet in the good man's speech they were scarcely known. He did refer to them, but only incidentally. The hero of the hour was this boy. Did the nation owe him anything? No, nothing then and nothing now. Why was he called the hero? Simply because that speaker fell into that same human error—that this boy was great because he was an officer and the others were only private soldiers.

Oh, I learned the lesson then that I will never forget so long as the tongue of the bell of time continues to swing for me. **Greatness consists not in holding of some future office, but really consists in doing great deeds with little means and the accomplishment of vast purposes from the private ranks of life.** To be great at all one must be great here, now, in Philadelphia. He who can give to this city better streets and better sidewalks, better schools and more colleges, more happiness and more civilization, more of God, he will be great anywhere. **Let every man or woman** here, if you never hear me again, **remember this, that if you wish to be great at all you must begin where you are and what you are,** in Philadelphia, now. He that can give to his city any blessing, he who can be a good citizen while he lives here, he that can make better homes, he that can be a blessing whether he works in the shop or sits behind the counter or keeps house, whatever be his life, he who would be great anywhere must first be great in his own Philadelphia.

(End of Dr. Conwell's lecture).

The Author's Life and Achievements

by Robert Shackleton

1

The Story of the Sword

I shall write of a remarkable man, an interesting man, a man of power, of initiative, of will, of persistence; a man who plans vastly and who realizes his plans; a man who not only does things himself, but who, even more important than that, is the constant inspiration of others. I shall write of Russell H. Conwell.*

As a farmer's boy, he was the leader of the boys of the rocky region that was his home; as a school teacher, he won devotion; as a newspaper correspondent, he gained fame; as a soldier in the Civil War, he rose to important rank; as a lawyer, he developed a large practice; as an author, he wrote books that reached a mighty total of sales. He left the law for the ministry and is the active head of a great church that he raised from nothingness. He is the most popular lecturer in the world and yearly speaks to many thousands. **He is,** so to speak, **the discoverer of "Acres of Diamonds," a concept through which thousands of men and women have achieved success out of failure.** He is the head of two hospitals, one of them founded by himself, that have cared for a host of patients, both the poor and the rich, irrespective of race or creed. He is the founder and head of Temple University, that has already taught tens of thousands of students. His home is in Philadelphia, but he is known in every corner of every state in

---

*Dr. Conwell was living, and actively at work, when these pages were written. It is, therefore, a much truer picture of his personality than anything written in the past tense.

the Union, and everywhere he has hosts of friends. All of his life he has helped and inspired others.

Quite by chance, and only yesterday, with no thought at the moment of Conwell—although he had been much in my mind for some time past—I picked up a thin little book of description by William Dean Howells. Turning the pages of a chapter on Lexington, old Lexington of the Revolution, written in 1882, I noticed, after he had written of the town itself and of the long-past fight there, and of the present-day aspect, that he mentioned the church life of the place. He remarked on the striking advances made by the Baptists, who had lately, as he expressed it, been reconstituted out of perishing fragments and made strong and flourishing under the ministrations of a lay preacher, formerly a colonel in the Union army. It was only a few days before that I chanced upon this description that Dr. Conwell, the former colonel and former lay preacher, had given me of his experiences in that little old Revolutionary town.

Howells went on to say that the colonel's success was principally due to his making the church attractive to young people. Howells says no more of him; apparently he did not go to hear him. One wonders if he has ever associated that lay preacher of Lexington with the famous Russell H. Conwell of these recent years!

"Attractive to young people." Yes, one can recognize that today, just as it was recognized in Lexington. It may be added that he at the same time attracts older people, too! In this, indeed, lies his power. He makes his church interesting, his sermons interesting, his lectures interesting. He is himself interesting! Because of his being interesting, he gains attention. The attention gained, he inspires.

Biography is more than dates. Dates, after all, are but milestones along the road of life. The most important fact of Conwell's life is that he lived to be eighty-two, working sixteen hours every day for the good of his fellow men. He was born on February 15, 1843—born of poor parents, in a low-roofed cottage in the eastern Berkshires, in Massachusetts.

"I was born in this room," he said to me, simply, as we sat together recently* in front of the old fireplace in the principal room of the little cottage, for he has bought back the rocky farm of his father, and has retained and restored the little old home. "I was born in this room. It was bedroom and kitchen. It was poverty." And his voice sank with a kind of grimness into silence.

Then he spoke a little of the struggles of those long-past years. We went out on the porch as the evening shadows fell, and looked out over the valley and stream and hills of his youth, and he told of his grandmother, and of a young Marylander who had come to the region on a visit. It was a tale of the impetuous love of those two, of rash marriage, of the interference of parents, of the fierce rivalry of another suitor, of an attack on the Marylander's life, of passionate hastiness, of unforgivable words, of separation, of lifelong sorrow. "Why does grandmother cry so often?" he remembers asking when he was a little boy. And he was told that it was for the husband of her youth.

We went back into the little house, and he showed me the room in which he first saw John Brown. "I came down early one morning, and saw a huge, hairy man sprawled upon the bed there—and I was frightened," he says.

----

*This interview took place at the old Conwell farm in the summer of 1915.

But John Brown did not long frighten him! He was much at their house after that, and was so friendly with Russell and his brother that there was no chance for awe. It gives a curious sidelight on the character of the stern abolitionist that he actually, with infinite patience, taught the old horse of the Conwells to go home alone with the wagon after leaving the boys at school, a mile or more away, and at school-closing time to trot gently off for them without a driver, when merely faced in that direction and told to go! Conwell remembers how John Brown, in training it, would patiently walk beside the horse and control its going and its turnings, until it was quite ready to go and turn entirely by itself.

The Conwell house was a station on the Underground Railway, and Russell Conwell remembers, when a lad, seeing the escaping slaves that his father had driven across country and temporarily hidden. "Those were heroic days," he says, quietly. "And once in a while my father let me go with him. They were wonderful night drives—the cowering slaves, the darkness of the road, the caution and the silence and dread of it all." This underground route, he remembers, was from Philadelphia to New Haven, thence to Springfield, where Conwell's father would take his charge, and onward to Bellows Falls and Canada.

Conwell tells, too, of meeting Frederick Douglass, the colored orator, in that little cottage in the hills. "'I never saw my father,' Douglass said one day—his father was a white man—'and I remember little of my mother except that once she tried to keep an overseer from whipping me, and the lash cut across her own face, and her blood fell over me.'

"When John Brown was captured," Conwell went on, "my father tried to sell this place to get a little money to help his defense. But he couldn't sell it, and on the day of the execution we knelt solemnly here, from eleven to twelve, just praying, praying in silence for the passing of John Brown. As we prayed we knew that others were also praying, for a church bell tolled during that entire hour, and its awesome boom went sadly sounding over these hills."

Conwell believes that his real life dates from a happening in the time of the Civil War—a happening that still looms vivid and intense before him, and which undoubtedly did deepen and strengthen his strong and deep nature. Yet the real Conwell was always essentially the same. Neighborhood tradition still tells of his bravery as a boy and a youth, of his reckless coasting, his skill as a swimmer and his saving of lives, his strength and endurance, his plunging out into the darkness of a wild winter night to save a neighbor's cattle. His soldiers came home with tales of his devotion to them, and of how he shared his rations and his blankets and bravely risked his life; of how he crept off into a swamp, at imminent peril, to rescue one of his men lost or mired there. Today's Conwell was always Conwell. In fact, he may be traced through his ancestry, for in him are the sturdy virtues, the bravery, the grim determination, the practicality, of his father; the romanticism, that comes from his grandmother, and the dreamy qualities of his mother, who, practical and hardworking New England woman that she was, was at the same time influenced by an almost startling mysticism.

Conwell himself is a dreamer; first of all, he is a dreamer; it is the most important fact in regard to him! It is because he is a dreamer and visualizes his dreams that he can plan the great things that to other men would seem impossibilities. Then his intensely practical side—his intense efficiency, his power, his skill, his patience, his fine earnestness, his mastery over others, develop his dreams into realities. He dreams dreams and sees visions—but his visions are never visionary and his dreams become facts.

The rocky hills which meant a dogged struggle for very existence, the fugitive slaves, John Brown—what a school for youth! The physical school was a tiny one-room schoolhouse where young Conwell came under the care of a teacher who realized the boy's unusual capabilities and was able to give him broad and unusual help. Then a wise country preacher also recognized the unusual, and urged the parents to give still more education, whereupon a supreme effort was made and young Russell was sent to Wilbraham Academy. He likes to tell of his life there, of the hardships, of which he makes light, and of the joy with which weekend pies and cakes were received from home!

He tells of how he went out on the roads selling books from house to house, and of how eagerly he devoured the contents of the sample books he carried. "They were a foundation of learning for me," he says, soberly. "And they gave me a broad idea of the world."

He went to Yale in 1860, but the outbreak of the war interfered with college, and he enlisted in 1861. But he was only eighteen, and his father objected, and he went back to Yale. But next year he again enlisted, and men of his Berkshire neighborhood, likewise enlisting, insisted that he be their captain. Governor Andrews, appealed to, consented to commission the nineteen-year-old youth who was so evidently a natural leader. The men gave freely of their scant money to get for him a sword, all gay and splendid with gilt, and upon the sword was the declaration in stately Latin that, "True friendship is eternal."

With that sword is associated the most vivid, the most momentous experience of Russell Conwell's life.

That sword hangs at the head of Conwell's bed in his home in Philadelphia. Man of peace that he is, and minister of peace, that symbol of war has for over half a century been of infinite importance to him.

He told me the story as we stood together before that sword. As he told the story, speaking with quiet repression, but seeing it all and living it all just as vividly as if it had occurred but yesterday, "That sword meant so much to me," he murmured, and then he began the tale:

"A boy up there in the Berkshires, a neighbor's son, was John Ring. I call him a boy, for we all called him a boy, and we looked upon him as a boy, for he was under-sized and under-developed—so much so that he could not enlist.

"For some reason he was devoted to me, and he not only wanted to enlist, but he also wanted to be in the artillery company of which I was captain. I could only take him along as my servant. I didn't want a servant, but it was the only way to take poor little Johnnie Ring.

"Johnnie was deeply religious, and would read the Bible every evening, before turning in. In those days I was an atheist, or at least thought I was, and I used to laugh at Ring, and after a while he took to reading the Bible outside the tent on account of my laughing at him! But he did not stop reading it, and his faithfulness to me remained unchanged.

"The scabbard of the sword was too glittering for the regulations"—the ghost of a smile hovered on Conwell's lips—"and I could not wear it, and could only wear a plain one for service and keep this hanging in my tent on the tent-pole. John Ring used to handle it adoringly, and kept it polished to brilliancy. It's dull enough these many years," he added somberly. To Ring it represented not only his captain, but the very glory and pomp of war.

"One day the Confederates suddenly stormed our position near New Berne and swept through the camp, driving our entire force before them. All, including my company, retreated hurriedly across the river, setting fire to a long wooden bridge as we went over. It soon blazed up furiously, making a barrier that the Confederates could not pass.

"Unknown to everybody, and unnoticed, John Ring had dashed back to my tent. I think he was able to make his way back because he looked like a mere boy. However that was, he got past the Confederates into my tent and took down, from where it was hanging on the tent-pole, my bright, gold-scabbarded sword.

"John Ring seized the sword that had long been so precious to him. He dodged here and there, and actually managed to gain the bridge just as it was beginning to blaze. He started across. The flames were every moment getting fiercer, the smoke denser, and now and then, as he crawled and staggered on, he leaned for a few seconds far over the bridge in an effort to get air. Both sides saw him; both sides watched his terrible progress, even while firing was fiercely kept up from each side of the river. And then a Confederate officer—he was one of General Pickett's officers—ran to the water's edge and waved a white handkerchief and the firing ceased.

"'Tell that boy to come back here!' he cried. 'Tell him to come back here and we will let him go free!'

"He called this out just as Ring was about to enter upon the worst part of the bridge—the covered part, where there were top and bottom and sides of blazing wood. The roar of the flames was so close to Ring that he could not hear the calls from either side of the river, and he pushed desperately on and disappeared in the covered part.

"There was dead silence except for the crackling of the fire. Not a man cried out. All waited in hopeless expectancy. And then came a mighty yell from Northerner and Southerner alike, for Johnnie came crawling out of the end of the covered way—he had actually passed through that frightful place—and his clothes were ablaze, and he toppled over and fell into shallow water. In a few moments he was dragged out unconscious, and hurried to a hospital.

"He lingered for a day or so, still unconscious, and then came to himself and smiled a little as he found that the sword for which he had given his life had been left beside him. He took it in his arms. He hugged it to his breast. He gave a few words of final message for me. And that was all."

Conwell's voice had gone thrillingly low as he neared the end, for it was all so very, very vivid to him, and his eyes had grown tender and his lips more strong and firm. And he fell silent, thinking of that long-ago happening, and though he looked down upon the thronging traffic of Broad Street, it was clear that he did not see it, and that if the rumbling hubbub of sound meant anything to him it was the rumbling of the guns of the distant past. When he spoke again, it was with a still tenser tone of feeling.

"When I stood beside the body of John Ring and realized that he had died for love of me, I made a vow that has formed my life. I vowed that from that moment I would live not only my own life, but that I would also live the life of John Ring. And from that moment I have worked sixteen hours every day—eight for John Ring's work and eight hours for my own."

A curious note had come into his voice, as of one who had run the race and neared the goal, fought the good fight and neared the end.

"Every morning when I rise I look at this sword, or if I am away from home I think of the sword, and vow anew that another day shall see sixteen hours of work from me."

When one comes to know Russell Conwell he realizes that never did a man work harder and more constantly.

"It was through John Ring and his giving his life through devotion to me that I became a Christian," he went on. "This did not come about immediately, but it came before the war was over, and it came through faithful Johnnie Ring."

There is a little, lonely cemetery in the Berkshires, a tiny burying ground on a windswept hill, a few miles from Conwell's old home. In this isolated burying ground, bushes and vines and grass grow in profusion, a few trees cast a gentle shade, and tree-clad hills go billowing off for miles and miles in wild and lonely beauty. In that lonely, little graveyard I found the plain stone that marks the resting place of John Ring.

2

The Beginning at Old Lexington

It is not because he is a minister that Russell Conwell is such a force in the world. He went into the ministry because he was sincerely and profoundly a Christian, and because he felt that as a minister he could do more good in the world than in any other capacity. But being a minister is but an incident, so to speak. The important thing is not that he is a minister, but that he is himself!

Recently I heard a New Yorker, the head of a great corporation, say: "I believe that Russell Conwell is doing more good in the world than any other man who has lived since Jesus Christ." He said this in serious and unexaggerated earnest.

Yet Conwell did not get readily into his lifework. He might have seemed almost a failure until he was well on toward forty, for although he kept making successes they were not permanent successes, and he did not settle himself into a definite line. He restlessly went westward to make his home, and then restlessly returned to the East. After the war was over, he was a lawyer, a lecturer, an editor. He went around the world as a correspondent; he wrote books. He kept making money, and kept losing it; he lost it through fire, through investments, through aiding his friends. It is probable that the unsettledness of the years following the war was due to the unsettling effect of the war itself, which thus, in its influence, broke into his

mature life after breaking into his years at Yale. But however that may be, those seething, changing, stirring years
were years of vital importance to him, for in the myriad
experiences of that time he was building the foundation of
the Conwell that was to come. Abroad he met the notables
of the earth. At home he attracted hosts of friends and
loyal admirers.

It is worthwhile noting that as a lawyer he would
never take a case, either civil or criminal, that he considered wrong. It was basic with him that he could not and
would not fight on what he thought was the wrong side.
Only when his client was right would he go ahead!

Yet he laughs, his quiet, infectious, characteristic laugh,
as he tells of how once he was deceived, for he defended a
man, charged with stealing a watch, who was so obviously
innocent that he took the case in a blaze of indignation and
had the young fellow proudly exonerated. The next day
the "wrongly accused" one came to his office and shame-
facedly took out the watch that he had been charged with
stealing. "I want you to send it to the man I took it from,"
he said. He told with a sort of shamefaced pride of how he
had got a good old deacon to give, in all sincerity, the
evidence that exculpated him. "And, say, Mr. Conwell—I
want to thank you for getting me off and I hope you'll
excuse my deceiving you—I won't be any worse for not
going to jail." Conwell likes to remember that thereafter
the young man lived up to the pride of exoneration. Though
Conwell does not say it or think it, one knows that it was
the Conwell influence that inspired to honesty—for always
he is an inspirer.

Conwell even kept certain hours for consultation with
those too poor to pay any fee. At one time, while still an
active lawyer, he was guardian for over sixty children! The

man has always been a marvel, and always one is coming upon such romantic facts as these.

That is a curious thing about him—how much there is of romance in his life! Worshipped to the end by John Ring; left for dead all night at Kenesaw Mountain; calmly singing "Nearer, my God, to Thee," to quiet the passengers on a supposedly sinking ship; saving lives even when a boy; never disappointing a single audience of the thousands of audiences he had arranged to address during all his years of lecturing! He himself takes a little pride in this last point, and it is characteristic of him that he has actually forgotten that just once he did fail to appear. He has quite forgotten that one evening, on his way to a lecture, he stopped a runaway horse to save two women's lives, and went in consequence to a hospital instead of to the platform! And it is typical of him to forget that sort of thing.

The emotional temperament of Conwell has always made him responsive to the great, the striking, the patriotic. He was deeply influenced by knowing John Brown, and his brief memories of Lincoln are intense, though he saw him but three times in all.

The first time he saw Lincoln was on the night when the future President delivered the address, which afterward became so famous, in Cooper Union, New York. The name of Lincoln was then scarcely known, and it was by mere chance that young Conwell happened to be in New York on that day. But being there, and learning that Abraham Lincoln from the West was going to make an address, he went to hear him.

He tells how uncouthly Lincoln was dressed, even with one trousers-leg higher than the other, and of how awkward he was, and of how poorly, at first, he spoke and with what apparent embarrassment. The chairman of the meeting got Lincoln a glass of water, and Conwell thought that it was from a personal desire to help him and keep him from breaking down. But he loves to tell how Lincoln became a changed man as he spoke; how he seemed to feel ashamed of his brief embarrassment and, pulling himself together and putting aside the written speech which he had prepared, spoke freely and powerfully, with splendid conviction, as only a born orator speaks. To Conwell it was a tremendous experience.

The second time he saw Lincoln was when he went to Washington to plead for the life of one of his men who had been condemned to death for sleeping on post. He was still but a captain (his promotion to a colonelcy was yet to come), a youth, and was awed by going into the presence of the man he worshipped. And his voice trembles a little, even now, as he tells of how pleasantly Lincoln looked up from his desk, and how cheerfully he asked his business with him, and of how absorbedly Lincoln then listened to his tale, although, so it appeared, he already knew of the main outline.

"It will be all right," said Lincoln, when Conwell finished. But Conwell was still frightened. He feared that in the multiplicity of public matters this mere matter of the life of a mountain boy, a private soldier, might be forgotten till too late. "It is almost the time set—" he faltered. And Conwell's voice almost breaks, man of emotion that he is, as he tells of how Lincoln said, with stern gravity: "Go and telegraph that soldier's mother that Abraham Lincoln never signed a warrant to shoot a boy under twenty, and never will." That was the one and only time that he spoke with Lincoln, and it remains an indelible impression.

The third time he saw Lincoln was when, as officer of the day, he stood for hours beside the dead body of the

President as it lay in state in Washington. In those hours, as he stood rigidly as the throng went shuffling sorrowfully through, an immense impression came to Colonel Conwell of the work and worth of the man who there lay dead, and that impression has never departed.

John Brown, Abraham Lincoln, old Revolutionary Lexington—how Conwell's life is associated with famous men and places! It was actually at Lexington that he made the crucial decision as to the course of his life.

It seems to me the very location of Lexington influenced Conwell to decide and to act as he did. Had it been in some other kind of place, some merely ordinary place, some quite usual place, he might not have taken the important step. But it was Lexington, it was brave old Lexington, inspiring Lexington. He was inspired by it, for the man who himself inspires nobly is always the one who is himself open to noble inspiration. Lexington inspired him.

"When I was a lawyer in Boston and almost thirty-seven years old," he told me, thinking slowly back into the years, "I was consulted by a woman who asked my advice in regard to disposing of a little church in Lexington whose congregation had become unable to support it. I went out and looked at the place, and I told her how the property could be sold. But it seemed a pity to me that the little church should be given up. However, I advised a meeting of the church members, and I attended the meeting. I put the case to them—it was only a handful of men and women—and there was silence for a little. Then an old man rose and, in a quavering voice, said the matter was quite clear, that there evidently was nothing to do but to sell, and that he would agree with the others in the necessity, but as the church had been his church home from boyhood (so he quavered and quivered on), he begged that they would excuse him from actually taking part in disposing of it, and in a deep silence he went haltingly from the room.

"The men and the women looked at one another, still silent, sadly impressed, but not knowing what to do. I said to them: 'Why not start over again, and go on with the church, after all!'"

Typical Conwellism, that! First, the impulse to help those who need helping, then the inspiration and leadership.

"'But the building is entirely too tumble-down to use,' said one of the men, sadly, and I knew he was right, for I had examined it, but I said:

"'Let us meet there tomorrow morning and get to work on that building ourselves and put it in shape for a service next Sunday.'

"It made them seem so pleased and encouraged, and so confident that a new possibility was opening that I never doubted that each one of those present, and many friends besides, would be at the building in the morning. I was there early with a hammer and ax and crowbar that I had secured, ready to go to work—but no one else showed up!"

He has a rueful appreciation of the humor of it, as he pictured the scene. One knows also that, in that little town of Lexington, where Americans had so bravely faced the impossible, Russell Conwell also braced himself to face the impossible. A pettier man would instantly have given up the entire matter when those who were most interested failed to respond, but one of the strongest features in Conwell's character is his ability to draw even doubters and weaklings into line, his ability to stir even those who have given up.

"I looked over that building," he goes on, whimsically, "and I saw that repair really seemed out of the question. Nothing but a new church would do! So I took the ax that I had brought with me and began chopping the place down. In a little while a man, not one of the church members, came along, and he watched me for a time and said, 'What are you going to do there?'

"And I instantly replied, 'Tear down this old building and build a new church here!'

"He looked at me. 'But the people won't do that,' he said.

"'Yes, they will,' I said, cheerfully, keeping at my work. He watched me a few minutes longer and said:

"'Well, you can put me down for one hundred dollars for the new building. Come up to my livery stable and get it this evening.'

"'All right; I'll surely be there,' I replied.

"In a little while another man came along and stopped and looked, and he rather gibed at the idea of a new church, and when I told him of the livery stable man contributing one hundred dollars, he said, 'But you haven't got the money yet!'

'No,' I said; 'but I am going to get it tonight.'

"'You'll never get it,' he said. 'He's not that sort of a man. He's not even a church man!'

"But I just went quietly on with the work without answering, and after quite a while he left, but he called back, as he went off: 'Well, if he does give you that hundred dollars, come to me and I'll give you another hundred.'"

Conwell smiles in genial reminiscence and without any apparent sense that he is telling of a great personal triumph, and goes on:

"Those two men both paid the money, and of course the church people themselves, who at first had not quite understood that I could be in earnest, joined in and helped, with work and money. While the new church was building, it was particularly important to get and keep the congregation together, and as they had ceased to have a minister of their own, I used to run out from Boston and preach for them, in a room we hired.

"And it was there in Lexington, in 1879, that I determined to become a minister. I had a good law practice, but I decided to give it up. For many years I had felt more or less of a call to the ministry, and here at length was the definite time to begin.

"Week by week I preached there." How strange, now, to think of William Dean Howells, and the Colonel-preacher!—"and after a while the church was completed, and in that very church, there in Lexington, I was ordained a minister."

A marvelous thing, all this, even without considering the marvelous heights that Conwell has since attained—a marvelous thing, an achievement of positive romance! That little church stood for American bravery and initiative and self-sacrifice and romanticism in a way that well befitted good old Lexington.

To leave a large and overflowing law practice and take up the ministry at a salary of six hundred dollars a year seemed to the relatives of Conwell's wife the extreme of foolishness, and they did not hesitate so to express themselves. Naturally enough, they did not have Conwell's vision. Yet he himself was fair enough to realize and to admit that there was a good deal of fairness in their objections. So he said to the congregation that, although he was quite ready to come for the six hundred dollars a year, he expected them to double his salary as soon as he doubled the church membership. This seemed to them a good deal like a joke, but they answered in perfect earnestness that they would be quite willing to do the doubling as soon as he did the doubling, and in less than a year the salary was doubled accordingly.

I asked him if he had found it hard to give up the lucrative law for a poor ministry, and his reply gave a delightful impression of his capacity for humorous insight into human nature, for he said, with a genial twinkle:

"Oh yes, it was a wrench, but there is a sort of romance in self-sacrifice, you know. I suppose the old-time martyrs rather enjoyed themselves in being martyrs!"

Conwell did not stay very long in Lexington. A struggling little church in Philadelphia heard of what he was doing, and so an old deacon went up to see and hear him, and an invitation was given. As the Lexington church seemed to be prosperously on its feet, and the needs of the Philadelphia body keenly appealed to Conwell's imagination, a change was made, and at a salary of eight hundred dollars a year he went, in 1882, to the little struggling Philadelphia congregation, and of that congregation he is still pastor—only, it ceased to be a struggling congregation a great many years ago! Long ago it began paying him more thousands every year than at first it gave him hundreds.

Dreamer as Conwell always is in connection with his immense practicality, and moved as he is by the spiritual influences of life, it is more than likely that not only did Philadelphia's need appeal, but also the fact that Philadelphia, as a city, meant much to him. Coming North, wounded from a battlefield of the Civil War, it was in Philadelphia that he was cared for until his health and strength were recovered. So it happened that Philadelphia had early become dear to him.

Here is an excellent example of how **dreaming great dreams may go hand-in-hand with winning superb results.** That little struggling congregation now owns and occupies a great new church building that seats more people than any other Protestant church in America—and Dr. Conwell fills it!

3

The Story of the Fifty-seven Cents

At every point in Conwell's life one sees that he wins through his wonderful personal influence on old and young. Every step forward, every triumph achieved, comes not alone from his own enthusiasm, but because of his putting that enthusiasm into others. And when I learned how it came about that the present church buildings were begun, it was another of those marvelous tales of fact that are stranger than any imagination could make them. And yet the tale was so simple and sweet and sad and unpretending.

When Dr. Conwell first assumed charge of the little congregation that led him to Philadelphia, it was really a little church both in its numbers and in the size of the building that it occupied, but it quickly became so popular under his leadership that the church services and Sunday school services were alike so crowded that there was no room for all who came, and always there were people turned from the doors.

One afternoon a little girl, who had eagerly wished to go, turned back from the Sunday school door, crying bitterly because they had told her that there was no more room. But a tall, black-haired man met her and noticed her tears and, stopping, asked why it was that she was crying, and she sobbingly replied that it was because they could not let her into the Sunday school.

"I lifted her to my shoulder," says Dr. Conwell, in telling of this, for after hearing the story elsewhere I asked him to tell it to me himself—it seemed almost too strange to be true. "I lifted her to my shoulder"—and one realizes the pretty scene it must have made for the little girl to go through the crowd of people, drying her tears and riding proudly on the shoulders of that kindly, tall man! "I said to her that I would take her in, and I did so, and I said to her that we should some day have a room big enough for all who should come. When she went home she told her parents (I only learned this afterward) that she was going to save money to help build the larger church and Sunday school that Dr. Conwell wanted! Her parents pleasantly humored her in the idea and let her run errands and do little tasks to earn pennies, and she began dropping the pennies into her bank.

"She was a lovable little thing—but in only a few weeks after that she was taken suddenly ill and died. At the funeral her father told me, quietly, of how his little girl had been saving money for a building fund. There, at the funeral, he handed me what she had saved—just fifty-seven cents in pennies."

Dr. Conwell does not say how deeply he was moved; he is, after all, a man of very few words as to his own emotions. But a deep tenderness had crept into his voice.

"At a meeting of the church trustees I told of this gift of fifty-seven cents—the first gift toward the proposed building fund of the new church of the future. Until then, the matter had barely been spoken of, as a new church building had been simply a future possibility.

"The trustees seemed much impressed, and it turned out that they were far more impressed than I could possibly have hoped, for in a few days one of them came to me and said that he thought it would be an excellent idea to buy a lot on Broad Street—the very lot on which the building now stands."

It was characteristic of Dr. Conwell that he did not point out what everyone who knows him would understand—that it was his own inspiration transferred to the trustees that resulted in this quick and definite move on the part of one of them. "I talked the matter over with the owner of the property, and told him of the beginning of the fund, the story of the little girl. The man was not one of our church, nor, in fact, was he a church-goer at all, but he listened attentively to the tale of the fifty-seven cents and simply said he was quite ready to go ahead and sell us that piece of land for ten thousand dollars, taking—and the unexpectedness of this deeply touched me—taking a first payment of just fifty-seven cents and letting the entire balance stand on a five per cent mortgage!

"And it seemed to me that it would be the right thing to accept this unexpectedly liberal proposition, and I went over the entire matter on that basis with the trustees and some of the other members, and all the people were soon talking of having a new church. But it was not done in that way, after all, for, fine though that way would have been, there was to be one still finer.

"Not long after my talk with the man who owned the land, and his surprisingly good-hearted proposition, an exchange was arranged for me one evening with a Mount Holly church, and my wife went with me. We came back late, and it was cold and wet and miserable, but as we approached our home, we saw that it was all lighted from top to bottom, and it was clear that it was full of people. I said to my wife that they seemed to be having a better time than we had had, and we went in, curious to know what it was all about. It turned out that our absence had been intentionally arranged, and that the church people had gathered at our home to meet us on our return. I was utterly amazed, for the spokesman told me that the entire ten thousand dollars had been raised and that the land for the church that I wanted was free of debt. And all had come so quickly and directly from that dear little girl's fifty-seven cents."

Doesn't it seem like a fairy tale! But then **this man has all his life been turning fairy tales into realities.** He inspired the child. He inspired the trustees. He inspired the owner of the land. He inspired the people.

The building of the great church—the Temple Baptist Church, as it is called—was a great undertaking for the congregation. Even though it had been swiftly growing from the day of Dr. Conwell's taking charge of it, it was something far ahead of what, except in the eyes of an enthusiast, they could possibly complete and pay for and support. Nor was it an easy task.

Ground was broken for the building in 1889; in 1891 it was opened for worship, and then came years of raising money to clear it. But it was long ago placed completely out of debt, and with only a single large subscription—one of ten thousand dollars, for the church is not in a wealthy neighborhood, nor is the congregation made up of the great and rich.

The church is built of stone, and its interior is a great amphitheater. Special attention has been given to fresh air and light; there is nothing of the dim, religious light that goes with medieval churches. Behind the pulpit are tiers of seats for the great chorus choir. There is a large organ. The building is peculiarly adapted for hearing and seeing, and if it is not, strictly speaking, beautiful in itself, it is beautiful when it is filled with encircling rows of men and women.

Man of feeling that he is, and one who appreciates the importance of symbols, Dr. Conwell had a heart of olive wood built into the front of the pulpit; the wood was from an olive tree in the Garden of Gethsemane. And the amber-colored tiles in the inner walls of the church bear, under the glaze, the names of thousands of his people. Every one, young or old, who helped in the building, even to the giving of a single dollar, has his name inscribed there. Dr. Conwell wished to show that it is not only the house of the Lord, but also, in a keenly personal sense, the house of those who built it.

The church has a possible seating capacity of 4,200, although only 3,135 chairs have been put in it, for it has been the desire not to crowd the space needlessly. There is also a great room for the Sunday school, and extensive rooms for the young men's association, the young women's association, for a kitchen, for executive offices, for meeting places for church officers and boards and committees. It is a spacious and practical and complete church home, and the people feel at home there.

"You see again," said Dr. Conwell, musingly, **"the advantage of aiming at big things.** That building represents $109,000 above ground. It is free from debt. Had we built a small church, it would now be heavily mortgaged."

4

His Power As Orator and Preacher

E ven as a young man Conwell won local fame as an
orator. At the outbreak of the Civil War he began
making patriotic speeches that gained enlistments. After
going to the front he was sent back home for a time, on
furlough, to make more speeches to draw more recruits,
for his speeches were so persuasive, so powerful, so full of
homely and patriotic feeling, that the men who heard them
thronged into the ranks. Also, as a preacher, he uses per-
suasion, power, simple and homely eloquence, to draw
people to the ranks of Christianity.

He is an orator born, and has developed this inborn
power by the hardest of study and thought and practice.
He is one of those rare men who always seizes and holds
the attention. When he speaks, men listen. It is quality,
temperament, control—the word is immaterial, but the fact
is very material indeed.

Some quarter of a century ago Conwell published a
little book for students on the study and practice of oratory. That **"clear-cut articulation is the charm of eloquence"**
is one of his insisted-upon statements, and it well illustrates the lifelong practice of the man himself. Every word
as he talks can be heard in every part of a large building,
yet always he speaks without apparent effort. He avoids
"elocution." His voice is soft-pitched and never breaks,
even now when he is over seventy, because, so he explains
it, he always speaks in his natural voice. There is never a
straining after effect.

"A speaker must possess a large-hearted regard for the welfare of his audience," he writes, and here again we see Conwell explaining Conwellism. **"Enthusiasm invites enthusiasm,"** is another of his points of importance. One understands that it is by deliberate purpose, and not by chance, that he tries with such tremendous effort to put enthusiasm into his hearers with every sermon and every lecture that he delivers.

"It is easy to raise a laugh, but dangerous, for it is the greatest test of an orator's control of his audience to be able to land them again on the solid earth of sober thinking." I have known him at the very end of a sermon have a ripple of laughter sweep freely over the entire congregation, and then in a moment he has every individual under his control, listening soberly to his words.

He never fears to use humor, and it is always very simple and obvious and effective. With him even a very simple pun may be used, not only without taking away from the strength of what he is saying, but with a vivid increase of impressiveness. And when he says something funny it is in such a delightful and confidential way, with a genial, quiet, infectious humorousness, that his audience is captivated. They never think that he is telling something funny of his own; it seems (such is the skill of the man) that he is just letting them know of something humorous that they are to enjoy with him.

"Be absolutely truthful and scrupulously clear," he writes. With delightfully terse common sense, he says, **"Use illustrations that illustrate"**—and never did an orator live up to this injunction more than does Conwell himself. Nothing is more surprising, nothing is more interesting, than the way in which he makes use as illustrations of the impressions and incidents of his long and varied life. Whatever it is, it has direct and instant bearing on the progress of his discourse. He will refer to something that he heard a child say in a train yesterday; in a few minutes he will speak of something that he saw or someone whom he met last month, or last year, or ten years ago—in Ohio, in California, in London, in Paris, in New York, in Bombay. Each memory, each illustration, is a hammer with which he drives home a truth.

The vast number of places he has visited and people he has met, the infinite variety of things his observant eyes have seen, give him his ceaseless flow of illustrations, and his memory and his skill make admirable use of them. It is seldom that he uses an illustration from what he has read; everything is, characteristically, his own. Henry M. Stanley, who knew him well, referred to him as "that double-sighted Yankee," who could "see at a glance all there is and all there ever was."

Never was there a man who so supplements with personal reminiscence the place or the person that has figured in the illustration. When he illustrates with the story of the discovery of California gold at Sutter's he almost parenthetically remarks, "I delivered this lecture on that very spot a few years ago—that is, in the town that arose on that very spot." When he illustrates with the story of the invention of the sewing machine, he adds: "I suppose that if any of you were asked who was the inventor of the sewing machine, you would say that it was Elias Howe. But that would be a mistake. I was with Elias Howe in the Civil War, and he told me how he had tried for fourteen years to invent the sewing machine and that then his wife, feeling that something really had to be done, invented it in a couple of hours." Listening to him, you begin to feel in touch with everybody and everything, and in a friendly and intimate way.

Always, whether in the pulpit or on the platform, as in private conversations, there is an absolute simplicity about the man and his words, **a simplicity, an earnestness, a complete honesty.** And when he sets down, in his book on oratory, **"A man has no right to use words carelessly,"** he stands for that respect for word-craftsmanship that every successful speaker or writer must feel.

"Be intensely in earnest," he writes, and in writing this he sets down a prime principle not only of his oratory, but of his life.

A young minister told me that Dr. Conwell once said to him, with deep feeling, "Always remember, as you preach, that you are striving to save at least one soul with every sermon." And to one of his close friends Dr. Conwell said, in one of his self-revealing conversations:

"I feel, whenever I preach, that there is always one person in the congregation to whom, in all probability, I shall never preach again, and therefore I feel that I must exert my utmost power in that last chance." Even if this were all, one sees why each of his sermons is so impressive, and why his energy never lags. **Always, with him, is the feeling that he is in the world to do all the good he can possibly do— not a moment, not an opportunity, must be lost.**

The moment he rises and steps to the front of his pulpit he has the attention of everyone in the building, and this attention he closely holds until he is through. Yet it is never by a striking effort that attention is gained, except insofar that his utter simplicity is striking. "I want to preach so simply that you will not think it preaching, but merely that you are listening to a friend," I remember his saying, one Sunday morning, as he began his sermon. Then he went on so simply, as such homely, kindly, friendly words promised. And how effectively!

He believes that everything should be so put as to be understood by all, and this belief he applies not only to his preaching, but to the reading of the Bible, whose descriptions he not only visualizes to himself, but makes vividly clear to his hearers; this often makes for fascination in result.

For example, he is reading the tenth chapter of I Samuel, and begins, "'Thou shalt meet a company of prophets.'"

"'Singers,' it should be translated," he puts in, lifting his eyes from the page and looking out over his people. Then he goes on, taking this change as a matter of course, "'Thou shalt meet a company of singers coming down from the high place—.'"

Here he again interrupts himself, and in an irresistible explanatory aside, which instantly raises the desired picture in the mind of everyone, he says: "That means, from the little old church on the hill, you know." How plain and clear and real and interesting—most of all, interesting—it is from this moment! Another man would have left it that prophets were coming down from a high place, which would not have seemed at all alive or natural, and here, suddenly, Conwell has flashed his picture of the singers coming down from the little old church on the hill! There is magic in doing that sort of thing.

And he goes on, now reading: "'Thou shalt meet a company of singers coming down from the little old church on the hill, with a psaltery, and a tabret, and a pipe, and a harp, and they shall sing.'"

Music is one of Conwell's strongest aids. He sings himself—sings as if he likes to sing, and often finds himself leading the singing—usually so, indeed, at the prayer meetings, and often, in effect at the church services.

I remember at one church service that the choir leader was standing in front of the massed choir ostensibly leading the singing, but that Conwell himself, standing at the rear of the pulpit platform, with his eyes on his hymn book, silently swaying a little with the music and unconsciously beating time as he swayed, was just as unconsciously the real leader, for it was he whom the congregation was watching and with him that they were keeping time! He never suspected it; he was merely thinking along with the music. There was such a look of contagious happiness on his face as made everyone in the building similarly happy, for he possesses a mysterious faculty of imbuing others with his own happiness.

Not only singers, but the modern equivalent of psaltery and tabret and cymbals, all have their place in Dr. Conwell's scheme of church service, for there may be a piano, even a trombone, and a great organ to help the voices, and at times there are chiming bells. His musical taste seems to tend toward the thunderous—or perhaps it is only that he knows there are times when people like to hear the thunderous and are moved by it.

And how the singers in the choir like it! They occupy a great curving space behind the pulpit, and put their hearts into song. As the congregation disperses and the choir filters down, sometimes they are still singing and some of them continue to sing as they go slowly out toward the doors. They are happy—Conwell himself is happy—all the congregation is happy. He makes everybody feel happy in coming to church. He makes the church attractive, just as Howells was so long ago told that he did in Lexington.

And there is something more than happiness; there is a sense of ease, of comfort, of general joy, that is quite unmistakable. There is nothing of stiffness or constraint, and with it all there is full reverence. It is no wonder that he is accustomed to fill every seat of the great building.

His gestures are usually very simple. Now and then, when he works up to emphasis, he strikes one fist in the palm of the other hand. When he is through you do not remember that he has made any gestures at all, but the sound of his voice remains with you, and the look of his wonderful eyes. Though he is past the threescore years and ten, he looks out over his people with eyes that still have the veritable look of youth.

Like all great men, he not only does big things, but keeps in touch with myriad details. When his assistant, announcing the funeral of an old member, hesitates about the street and number and says that they can be found in the telephone directory, Dr. Conwell's deep voice breaks quietly in with, "Such a number [giving it], Dauphin Street"—quietly, and in a low tone, yet everyone in the church hears distinctly every syllable of that low voice.

His fund of personal anecdote, or personal reminiscence, is constant and illustrative in his preaching, just as it is when he lectures, and the reminiscences sweep through many years, and at times are really startling in the vivid and homelike pictures they present of the famous folk of the past that he knew.

One Sunday evening he made an almost casual reference to the time when he first met Garfield, then a candidate for the Presidency. "I asked Major McKinley, whom I had met in Washington, and whose home was in northern Ohio, as was that of Mr. Garfield, to go with me to Mr. Garfield's home and introduce me. When we got there, a neighbor had to find him. 'Jim! Jim!' he called. You see, Garfield was just plain 'Jim' to his old neighbors. It's hard to recognize a hero over your back fence!" He paused a moment for the appreciative ripple to subside, and went on:

"We three talked there together"—what a rare talking that must have been—McKinley, Garfield, and Conwell—"we talked together, and after a while we got to the subject of hymns, and those two great men both told me how deeply they loved the old hymn, 'The Old-Time Religion.' Garfield especially loved it, so he told us, because the good old man who brought him up as a boy and to whom he owed such gratitude, used to sing it at the pasture bars outside of the boy's window every morning, and young Jim knew, whenever he heard that old tune, that it meant it was time for him to get up. He said that he had heard the best concerts and the finest operas in the world, but had never heard anything he loved as he still loved 'The Old-Time Religion.' I forget what reason there was for McKinley's especially liking it, but he, as did Garfield, liked it immensely."

What followed was a striking example of Conwell's intentness on losing no chance to fix an impression on his hearers' minds, and at the same time it was a really astonishing proof of his power to move and sway. A new expression came over his face, and he said, as if the idea had only at that moment occurred to him—as it most probably had—"I think it's in our hymnal!" And in a moment he announced the number, and the great organ struck up, and every person in the great church—every man, woman, and child— joined in the swinging rhythm of verse after verse, as if they could never tire, of "The Old-Time Religion." It is a simple melody—barely more than a single line of almost monotone music:

It was good enough for mother and it's good enough for me!
It was good in the fiery furnace and it's good enough for me!

Thus it went on, with never-wearying iteration, and each time with the refrain, more and more rhythmic and swaying:

The old-time religion,
The old-time religion,
The old-time religion—
It's good enough for me!

That it was good for the Hebrew children, that it was good for Paul and Silas, that it will help you when you're dying, that it will show the way to heaven—all these and still other lines were sung, with a sort of wailing softness, a curious monotone, a depth of earnestness. The man who had worked this miracle of control by evoking out of the past his memory of a meeting with two of the vanished great ones of the earth, stood before his people, leading them, singing with them, his eyes aglow with an inward light. His magic had suddenly set them into the spirit of the old camp-meeting days, the days of pioneering and hardship, when religion meant so much to everybody, and even those who knew nothing of such things felt them, if but vaguely. Every heart was moved and touched, and that old tune will sing in the memory of all who thus heard it, and as long as they live.

5

A Gift for Inspiring Others

The constant earnestness of Conwell, his desire to let no chance slip by without helping a fellow man, puts often into his voice, when he preaches, a note of eagerness, of anxiety. But when he prays, when he turns to God, his manner undergoes a subtle and unconscious change. A load has slipped off his shoulders and has been assumed by a higher power. Into his bearing, dignified though it was, there comes an unconscious increase of the dignity. Into his voice, firm as it was before, there comes a deeper note of firmness. He is apt to fling his arms widespread as he prays, in a fine gesture that he never uses at other times, and he looks upward with the dignity of a man who, talking to a higher being, is proud of being a friend and confidant. One does not need to be a Christian to appreciate the beauty and fineness of Conwell's prayers.

He is likely at any time to do the unexpected, and is so great a man and has such control that whatever he does seems to everybody a perfectly natural thing. His sincerity is so evident, and whatever he does is done simply and naturally, that it is just a matter of course.

I remember, during one church service, while the singing was going on, that he suddenly rose from his chair and, kneeling beside it, on the open pulpit, with his back to the congregation, remained in that posture for several minutes. No one thought it strange. I was likely enough the only one who noticed it. His people are used to his sincerities. And this time it was merely that he had a few words to say quietly to God and turned aside for a few moments to say them.

His earnestness of belief in prayer makes him a firm believer in answers to prayer, and, in fact, to what may be termed the direct interposition of Providence. Doubtless, the mystic strain inherited from his mother has much to do with this. He has a typically homely way of expressing it by one of his favorite maxims, one that he loves to repeat encouragingly to friends who are in difficulties themselves or who know of the difficulties that are his, and this heartening maxim is, **"Trust in God and do the next thing."**

At one time in the early days of his church work in Philadelphia a payment of a thousand dollars was absolutely needed to prevent a lawsuit in regard to a debt for the church organ. In fact, it was worse than a debt; it was a note signed by himself personally, that had become due— he was always ready to assume personal liability for debts of his church—and failure to meet the note would mean a measure of disgrace as well as marked church discouragement.

He had tried all the sources that seemed open to him, but in vain. He could not openly appeal to the church members, in this case, for it was in the early days of his pastorate, and his zeal for the organ, his desire and determination to have it, as a necessary part of church equipment, had outrun the judgment of some of his best friends, including that of the deacon who had gone to Massachusetts for him. They had urged a delay until other expenses were met, and he had acted against their advice.

He had tried such friends as he could, and he had tried prayer. But there was no sign of aid, whether supernatural or natural.

And then, literally on the very day on which the holder of the note was to begin proceedings against him, a check for precisely the needed one thousand dollars came to him, by mail, from a man in the West—a man who was a total stranger to him. It turned out that the man's sister, who was one of the Temple membership, had written to her brother of Dr. Conwell's work. She knew nothing of any special need for money, knew nothing whatever of any note or of the demand for a thousand dollars. She merely outlined to her brother what Dr. Conwell was accomplishing, and with such enthusiasm that the brother at once sent the opportune check.

At a later time the sum of ten thousand dollars was importunately needed. It was due, payment had been promised. It was for some of the construction work of the Temple University buildings. The last day had come, and Conwell and the very few who knew of the emergency were in the depths of gloom. It was too large a sum to ask the church people to make up, for they were not rich and they had already been giving splendidly, of their slender means, for the church and then for the university. There was no rich man to turn to; the men famous for enormous charitable gifts have never let themselves be interested in any of the work of Russell Conwell. It would be unkind and gratuitous to suggest that it has been because their names could not be personally attached, or because the work is of an unpretentious kind among unpretentious people. It need merely be said that neither they nor their agents have cared to aid, except that one of the very richest, whose name is the most distinguished in the entire world as a giver, did once, in response to a strong personal application, give thirty-five hundred dollars, this being the extent of the association of the wealthy with any of the varied Conwell works.

So when it was absolutely necessary to have ten thousand dollars, the possibilities of money had been exhausted, whether from congregation or individuals.

Russell Conwell, in spite of his superb optimism, is also a man of deep depressions, and this is because of the very fire and fervor of his nature, for always in such a nature there is balancing. **He believes in success; success must come!—success is in itself almost a religion with him—success for himself and for all the world who will try for it!** But there are times when he is sad and doubtful over some particular possibility. And **he intensely believes in prayer—faith can move mountains, but always he believes that it is better not to wait for the mountains thus to be moved, but to go right out and get to work at moving them.** Once in a while there comes a time when the mountain looms too threatening, even after the bravest efforts and the deepest trust. Such a time had come—the ten thousand dollar debt was a looming mountain that he had tried in vain to move. He could still pray, and he did, but it was one of the times when he could only think that something had gone wrong.

The dean of the university, who has been closely in touch with all his work for many years, told me how, in a discouragement which was the more notable through contrast with his usual unfailing courage, he left the executive offices for his home, a couple of blocks away.

"He went away with everything looking dark before him. It was Christmas time, but the very fact of its being Christmas only added to his depression—Christmas was such an unnatural time for unhappiness! But in a few minutes he came flying back, radiant, overjoyed, sparkling with happiness, waving a slip of paper in his hand which was a check for precisely ten thousand dollars! For he had just drawn it out of an envelope handed to him as he reached home, by the mail carrier.

"And it had come so strangely and so naturally! For the check was from a woman who was profoundly interested in his work, and who had sent the check knowing that in a general way it was needed, but without the least idea that there was any immediate need. That was eight or nine years ago, but although the donor was told at the time that Dr. Conwell and all of us were most grateful for the gift, it was not until very recently that she was told how opportune it was. And the change it made in Dr. Conwell! He is a great man for maxims, and all of us who are associated with him know that one of his favorites is that **'It will all come out right sometime!'** Of course we had a rare opportunity to tell him that he ought never to be discouraged. And it is so seldom that he is!"

When the big new church was being built, the members of the church were vaguely disturbed by noticing that when the structure reached the second story, at that height, on the side toward the vacant and unbought land adjoining, there were several doors built that opened literally into nothing but space!

When asked about these doors and their purpose, Dr. Conwell would make some casual reply, generally to the effect that they might be excellent as fire escapes. To no one, for quite a while, did he broach even a hint of the great plan that was forming in his mind, which was that the buildings of a university were some day to stand on that land immediately adjoining the church!

At that time the university, the Temple University as it is now called, was not even a college, although it was probably called a college. Conwell had organized it, and it consisted of a number of classes and teachers, meeting in highly inadequate quarters in two little houses. But the imagination of Conwell early pictured great new buildings with accommodations for thousands! In time the dream was realized, the imagination became a fact, and now those second floor doors actually open from the Temple Church into the Temple University!

You see, he always thinks big! He dreams big dreams and wins big success. **All his life he has talked and preached success, and it is a real and very practical belief with him that it is just as easy to do a large thing as a small one, and, in fact, a little easier!** And so he naturally does not see why one should be satisfied with the small things of life. "If your rooms are big the people will come and fill them," he likes to say. The same effort that wins a small success should, rightly directed, have won a great success. **"Think big things and then do them!"**

Most favorite of all maxims with this man of maxims, is *"Let Patience have her perfect work."* Over and over he loves to say it, and his friends laugh about his love for it, and he knows that they do and laughs about it himself. "I tire them all," he says, "for they hear me say it every day."

He says it every day because it means so much to him. It stands, in his mind, as a constant warning against anger or impatience or over-haste—faults to which his impetuous temperament is prone, though few have ever seen him either angry or impatient or hasty, so well does he exercise self-control. Those who have long known him well have said to me that they have never heard him censure anyone, that his forbearance and kindness are wonderful.

He is a sensitive man beneath his composure; he has suffered, and keenly, when he has been unjustly attacked; he feels pain of that sort for a long time, too, for even the passing of years does not entirely deaden it.

"When I have been hurt, or when I have talked with annoying cranks, I have tried to let Patience have her perfect work, for those very people, if you have patience with them, may afterward be of help."

And he went on to talk a little of his early years in Philadelphia, and he said, with sadness, that it had pained him to meet with opposition, and that it had even come from ministers of his own denomination, for he had been so misunderstood and misjudged. However, he added, (the momentary somberness lifting), even his bitter enemies had been won over with patience.

I could understand a good deal of what he meant, for one of the Baptist ministers of Philadelphia had said to me, with some shame, that at first it used actually to be the case that when Dr. Conwell would enter one of the regular ministers' meetings, all would hold aloof, not a single one stepping forward to meet or greet him.

"And it was all through our jealousy of his success," said the minister, vehemently. "He came to this city a stranger, and he won instant popularity, and we couldn't stand it, and so we pounced upon things that he did that were altogether unimportant. The rest of us were so jealous of his winning throngs that we couldn't see the good in him. And it hurt Dr. Conwell so much that for ten years he did not come to our conferences. But all this was changed long ago. Now no minister is so welcomed as he is, and I don't believe that there ever has been a single time since he started coming again that he hasn't been asked to say something to us. We got over our jealousy long ago and we all love him."

Nor is it only that the clergymen of his own denomination admire him, for not long ago, such having been Dr. Conwell's triumph in the city of his adoption, the rector of the most powerful and aristocratic church in Philadelphia voluntarily paid lofty tribute to his aims and ability, his work and his personal worth. "He is an inspiration to his brothers in the ministry of Jesus Christ," so this Episcopalian rector wrote. **"He is a friend to all that is good, a foe to all that is evil, a strength to the weak, a comforter to the sorrowing, a man of God.** These words come from the heart of one who loves, honors, and reverences him for his character and his deeds."

Dr. Conwell did some beautiful and unusual things in his church, instituted some beautiful and unusual customs, and one can see how narrow and hasty criticisms charged him, long ago, with sensationalism—charges long since forgotten except through the hurt still felt by Dr. Conwell himself. "They used to charge me with making a circus of the church—as if it were possible for me to make a circus of the church!" And his tone was one of grieved amazement after all these years.

He was original and he was popular, and therefore there were misunderstandings and jealousy. His Easter services, for example, years ago, became widely talked of and eagerly anticipated because each sermon would be wrought around some fine symbol. He would hold in his hand, in the pulpit, the blue robin's egg, or the white dove, or the stem of lilies, or whatever he had chosen as the particular symbol for the particular sermon, and that symbol would give him the central thought for his discourse, accented as it would be by the actual symbol itself in view of the congregation. The cross lighted by electricity, to shine down over the baptismal pool, the little stream of water cascading gently down the steps of the pool during the baptismal rite, the roses floating in the pool and his gift of one of them to each of the baptized as he or she left the water—all such things did seem, long ago, so unconventional. Yet his own people recognized the beauty and poetry of them, and thousands of Bibles in Philadelphia have a baptismal rose from Dr. Conwell pressed within the pages.

His constant individuality of mind, his constant freshness, alertness, brilliancy, warmth, sympathy, endear him to his congregation, and when he returns from an absence they bubble and effervesce over him as if he were some brilliant new preacher just come to them. He is always new to them. Were it not that he possesses some remarkable quality of charm he would long ago have become, so to speak, an old story, an always entertaining and delightful story, after all these years.

It is not only that they still throng to hear him either preach or lecture, though that itself would be noticeable, but it is the delightful and delighted spirit with which they do it. Just the other evening I heard him lecture in his own church, just after his return from an absence, and every face beamed happily up at him to welcome him back, and everyone listened as intently to his every word as if he had never been heard there before. When the lecture was over, a huge bouquet of flowers was handed up to him, and someone embarrassedly said a few words about its being because he was home again. It was all as if he had just returned from an absence of months—and he had been away just five and half days!

ABOU BEN ADHEM

Abou Ben Adhem (may his tribe increase!)
Awoke one night from a deep dream of peace,
And saw, within the moonlight in his room,
Making it rich, and like a lily in bloom,
An Angel writing in a book of gold:
Exceeding peace had made Ben Adhem bold,
And to the Presence in the room he said,
"What writest thou?" The Vision raised its head,
And with a look made of all sweet accord
Answered, "The names of those who love the Lord."
"And is mine one?" said Abou. "Nay, not so,"
Replied the Angel. Abou spoke more low
But cheerily still; and said, "I pray thee, then,
Write me as one that loves his fellow men."

The Angel wrote, and vanished. The next night
It came again with a great wakening light,
And showed the names whom love of God had blessed,
And, lo! Ben Adhem's name led all the rest!

(James Henry) Leigh Hunt

6

Millions of Hearers

That Conwell is not primarily a minister—that he is a minister because he is a sincere Christian, that he is first of all an Abou Ben Adhem,* a man who loves his fellow men, becomes more and more apparent as the scope of his lifework is recognized. One almost comes to think that his pastorate of a great church is even a minor matter beside the combined importance of his educational work, his lecture work, his hospital work, his work in general as a helper to those who need help.

For my own part, I should say that he is like some of the old-time prophets, the strong ones who found a great deal to attend to in addition to matters of religion. The power, the ruggedness, the physical and mental strength, the positive grandeur of the man—all these are like the general conceptions of the big Old Testament prophets. The suggestion is given only because it has often recurred, and therefore with the feeling that there is something more than fanciful in the comparison. Yet, after all, the comparison fails in one important particular, for none of the prophets seems to have had a sense of humor!

It is perhaps better and more accurate to describe him as the last of the old school of American philosophers, the last of those sturdy-bodied, high-thinking, achieving men

---

Abou Ben Adhem is the title of a poem by Leigh Hunt, about Abou Ben Adhem's vision of an angel who teaches that love for mankind is love for God. It is reproduced on the previous page.

who, in the old days, did their best to set American humanity in the right path—such men as Emerson, Alcott, Gough, Wendell Phillips, Garrison, Bayard Taylor, Beecher, men whom Conwell knew and admired in the long ago, and all of whom have long since passed away.

Conwell, in his going up and down the country, inspiring his thousands and thousands, is the survivor of that old-time group who used to travel about, dispensing wit and wisdom and philosophy and courage to the crowded benches of country lyceums, and the chairs of school houses and town halls, or the larger and more pretentious gathering-places of the cities.

Conwell himself is amused to remember that he wanted to talk in public from his boyhood, and that very early he began to yield to the inborn impulse. He laughs as he remembers the variety of country fairs and school commencements and anniversaries and even sewing circles where he tried his youthful powers, and all for experience alone, in the first few years, except possibly for such a thing as a ham or a jackknife! The first money that he ever received for speaking was, so he remembers with glee, seventy-five cents, and even that was not for his talk, but for horse hire! At the same time, there is more than amusement in recalling these experiences, for he knows that they were invaluable to him as training. For over half a century he has affectionately remembered John B. Gough, who, in the height of his own power and success, saw resolution and possibilities in the ardent young hill-man, and actually did him the kindness and the honor of introducing him to an audience in one of the Massachusetts towns. It was really a great kindness and a great honor, from a man who had won his fame to a young man just beginning an oratorical career.

Conwell's lecturing has been, considering everything, the most important work of his life, for by it he has come into close touch with so many millions—literally millions!—of people.

I asked him once if he had any idea how many he had talked to in the course of his career, and he tried to estimate how many thousands of times he had lectured, and the average attendance for each, but desisted when he saw that it ran into millions of hearers. What a marvel is such a fact as that! Millions of hearers!

I asked the same question of his private secretary, and found that no one had ever kept any sort of record, but as careful an estimate as could be made gave a conservative result of fully eight million hearers for his lectures, and adding the number to whom he has preached, who have been over five million, there is a total of well over thirteen million who have listened to Russell Conwell's voice! And this staggering total is, if anything, an underestimate. The figuring was done cautiously and was based upon such facts as that he now addresses an average of over forty-five hundred at his Sunday services (an average that would be higher were it not that his sermons in vacation time are usually delivered in little churches. When at home, at the Temple, he addresses three meetings every Sunday). He lectures throughout the entire course of each year, including six nights a week of lecturing during vacation time. What a power is wielded by a man who has held over thirteen million people under the spell of his voice! Probably no other man who ever lived had such a total of hearers. And the total is steadily mounting, for he is a man who has never known the meaning of rest.

I think it almost certain that Dr. Conwell has never spoken to any one of what, to me, is the finest point of his lecture work. It is that he still goes gladly and for small fees to the small towns that are never visited by other men of great reputation. He knows that it is the little places, the out-of-the-way places, the submerged places, that most need a pleasure and a stimulus, and he still goes out, man of well over seventy that he is, to tiny towns in distant states, heedless of the discomforts of traveling, of the poor little hotels that seldom have visitors, of the oftentimes hopeless cooking and the uncleanliness, of the hardships and the discomforts, of the unventilated and overheated or underheated halls. He does not think of claiming the relaxation earned by a lifetime of labor, or, if he ever does, the thought of the sword of John Ring restores instantly his fervid earnestness.

How he does it, how he can possibly keep it up, is the greatest marvel of all. I have before me a list of his engagements for the summer weeks of this year, 1915, and I shall set it down because it will specifically show, far more clearly than general statements, the kind of work he does. The list is the itinerary of his vacation. Vacation! Lecturing every evening but Sunday, and on Sundays preaching in the town where he happens to be!

June 24 Ackley, Ia.
June 25 Waterloo, Ia.
June 26 Decorah, Ia.
June 27 *Waukon, Ia.
June 28 Red Wing, Minn.
June 29 River Falls, Wis.
June 30 Northfield, Minn.
July 1 Faribault, Minn.
July 2 Spring Valley, Minn.
July 3 Blue Earth, Minn.
July 4 *Fairmount, Minn.
July 5 Lake Crystal, Minn.
July 6 Redwood Falls, Minn.
July 7 Willmer, Minn.

July 8 Dawson, Minn.
July 9 Redfield, S.D.
July 10 Huron, S.D.
July 11 *Brookings, S.D.
July 12 Pipestone, Minn.
July 13 Hawarden, Ia.
July 14 Canton, S.D.
July 15 Cherokee, Ia.
July 16 Pocahontas, Ia.
July 17 Glidden, Ia.
July 18 *Boone, Ia.
July 19 Dexter, Ia.
July 20 Indianola, Ia.
July 21 Corydon, Ia.

July 22 Essex, Ia.
July 23 Sidney, Ia.
July 24 Falls City, Nebr.
July 25 *Hiawatha, Kan.
July 26 Frankfort, Kan.
July 27 Greenleaf, Kan.
July 28 Osborne, Kan.
July 29 Stockton, Kan.
July 30 Phillipsburg, Kan.
July 31 Mankato, Kan.
En route to next date on
circuit.
Aug. 3 Westfield, Pa.
Aug. 4 Galston, Pa.
Aug. 5 Port Allegheny, Pa.
Aug. 6 Wellsville, N.Y.
Aug. 7 Bath, N.Y.
Aug. 8 *Bath, N.Y.
Aug. 9 Penn Yan, N.Y.
Aug. 10 Athens, N.Y.

Aug. 11 Owego, N.Y.
Aug. 12 Patchogue, L.I., N.Y.
Aug. 13 Port Jervis, N.Y.
Aug. 14 Honesdale, Pa.
Aug. 15 *Honesdale, Pa.
Aug. 16 Carbondale, Pa.
Aug. 17 Montrose, Pa.
Aug. 18 Tunkhannock, Pa.
Aug. 19 Nanticoke, Pa.
Aug. 20 Stroudsburg, Pa.
Aug. 21 Newton, N.J.
Aug. 22 *Newton, N.J.
Aug. 23 Hackettstown, N.J.
Aug. 24 New Hope, Pa.
Aug. 25 Doylestown, Pa.
Aug. 26 Phoenixville, Pa.
Aug. 27 Kennett, Pa.
Aug. 28 Oxford, Pa.
Aug. 29 *Oxford, Pa.
*Preach on Sunday.

All these hardships, all this traveling and lecturing, which would test the endurance of the youngest and strongest, **this man of over seventy assumes without receiving a particle of personal gain, for every dollar that he makes by it is given away in helping those who need helping.**

That Dr. Conwell is intensely modest is one of the curious features of his character. He sincerely believes that to write his life would be, in the main, just to tell what people have done for him. He knows and admits that he works unweariedly, but in profound sincerity he ascribes the success of his plans to those who have assisted him. It is in just this way that he looks upon every phase of his life. When he is reminded of the devotion of his old soldiers, he remembers it only with a sort of pleased wonder that they gave the devotion to him, and he quite forgets that they loved him because he was always ready to sacrifice ease or risk his own life for them.

He deprecates praise; if any one likes him, the liking need not be shown in words, but in helping along a good work. That his church has succeeded has been because of the devotion of the people; that the university has succeeded is because of the splendid work of the teachers and pupils; that the hospitals have done so much has been because of the noble services of physicians and nurses. To him, as he himself expresses it, realizing that success has come to his plans, it seems as if the realities are but dreams. He is astonished by his own success. He thinks mainly of his own shortcomings. "God and man have ever been very patient with me." His depression is at times profound when he compares the actual results with what he would like them to be, for **always his hopes have gone soaring far in advance of achievement. It is the "Hitch your chariot to a star" idea.**

His modesty goes hand-in-hand with kindliness, and I have seen him let himself be introduced in his own church to his congregation, when he is going to deliver a lecture there, just because a former pupil of the university was present who, Conwell knew, was ambitious to say something inside of the Temple walls, and this seemed to be the only opportunity.

I have noticed, when he travels, that the face of the newsboy brightens as he buys a paper from him, that the porter is all happiness, that conductor and brakeman are devotedly eager to be of aid. **Everywhere the man wins love. He loves humanity and humanity responds to the love.**

He has always won the affection of those who knew him, and Bayard Taylor was one of the many. He and

Bayard Taylor loved each other for long acquaintance and fellow experiences as world-wide travelers, back in the years when comparatively few Americans visited the Nile and the Orient, or even Europe.

When Taylor died there was a memorial service in Boston at which Conwell was asked to preside, and, as he wished for something more than addresses, he went to Longfellow and asked him to write and read a poem for the occasion. Longfellow had not thought of writing anything, and he was too ill to be present at the services, but, there always being something contagiously inspiring about Russell Conwell when he wishes something to be done, the poet promised to do what he could. And he wrote and sent the beautiful lines beginning:

> *Dead he lay among his books,*
> *The peace of God was in his looks.*

Many men of letters, including Ralph Waldo Emerson, were present at the services, and Dr. Conwell induced Oliver Wendell Holmes to read the lines, and they were listened to amid profound silence, to their fine ending.

Conwell, in spite of his widespread hold on millions of people, has never won fame, recognition, general renown, compared with many men of minor achievements. This seems like an impossibility, but is not—it is a fact. Great numbers of men of education and culture are entirely ignorant of him and his work in the world—men, these, who deem themselves in touch with world affairs and with the ones who make and move the world. It is inexplicable, this, except that never was there a man more devoid of the faculty of self-exploitation, self-advertising, than Russell Conwell. Nor, in the mere reading of them, do his words appeal with anything like the force of the same words uttered by himself, for always, with his spoken words, is his personality. Those who have heard Russell Conwell, or have known him personally, recognize the charm of the man and his immense forcefulness, but there are many, and among them those who control publicity through books and newspapers, who, though they ought to be the warmest in their enthusiasm, have never felt drawn to hear him, and, if they know of him at all, think of him as one who pleases in a simple way the commoner folk, forgetting in their pride that **every really great man pleases the common ones, and** that **simplicity and directness are attributes of real greatness.**

However, Russell Conwell has always won the admiration of the really great, as well as of the humbler millions. It is only a supposedly cultured class in between that is not thoroughly acquainted with what he has done.

Perhaps, too, this is owing to his having cast in his lot with the city, of all cities, which, consciously or unconsciously, looks most closely to family and place of residence as criteria of merit—a city with which it is almost impossible for a stranger to become affiliated—or aphiladelphiated, as it might be expressed—and Philadelphia, in spite of all that Dr. Conwell has done, has been under the thrall of the fact that he went north of Market Street—that fatal fact understood by all who know Philadelphia—and that he made no effort to make friends in Rittenhouse Square. Such considerations seem absurd in this twentieth century, but in Philadelphia they are still potent. Tens of thousands of Philadelphians love him, and he is honored by its greatest men, but there is a class of the pseudo-cultured who do not know him or appreciate him. It needs also to be understood that, outside of his own beloved Temple, he would prefer to go to a little church or a little hall and to speak to the forgotten people, in the hope of encouraging and inspiring them and filling them with hopeful glow, rather than to speak to the rich and comfortable.

His dearest hope, so one of the few who are close to him told me, **is that no one shall come into his life without being benefited.** He does not say this publicly, nor does he for a moment believe that such a hope could be fully realized, but it is very dear to his heart. No man spurred by such a hope, and thus bending all his thoughts toward the poor, the hard-working, the unsuccessful, is in a way to win honor from the Scribes, for we have Scribes now quite as much as when they were classed with Pharisees. It is not the first time in the world's history that Scribes have failed to give their recognition to one whose work was not among the great and wealthy.

That Conwell himself has seldom taken any part whatever in politics except as a good citizen standing for good government; that, as he expresses it, he never held any political office except that he was once on a school committee, and also that **he** does not identify himself with the so-called "movements" that from time to time catch public attention, but **aims only and constantly at the quiet betterment of mankind,** may be mentioned as additional reasons why his name and fame have not been steadily blazoned.

He knows and will admit that he works hard and has all his life worked hard. "Things keep turning my way because I'm on the job," as he whimsically expressed it one day, but that is about all, so it seems to him.

He sincerely believes that his life has in itself been without interest, that it has been an essentially commonplace life with nothing of the interesting or the eventful to tell. He is frankly surprised that there has ever been the desire to write about him. He really has no idea of how fascinating are the things he has done. His entire life has been of positive interest from the variety of things accomplished and the unexpectedness with which he has accomplished them.

Never, for example, was there such an organizer. In fact, organization and leadership have always been as the breath of life to him. While a youth, he organized debating societies and, before the war, a local military company. While on garrison duty in the Civil War he organized what is believed to have been the first free school for colored children in the South. One day Minneapolis was spoken of, and Conwell happened to remember that he organized, when he was a lawyer in that city, what became the first Y.M.C.A. branch there. Once he even started a newspaper. And it was natural that the organizing instinct, as years advanced, should lead him to greater and greater things, such as his church, with the numerous associations formed within itself through his influence, and the university—the organizing of the university being in itself an achievement of positive romance.

"A life without interest!" Why, when I happened to ask, one day, how many Presidents he had known since Lincoln, he replied, quite casually, that he had "written the lives of most of them in their own homes". By this he meant either personally or in collaboration with the American biographer Abbott.

The many-sidedness of Conwell is one of the things that is always fascinating. After you have quite got the feeling that he is peculiarly a man of today, lecturing on today's possibilities to the people of today, you happen upon some such fact as that he attracted the attention of *The Times* (London) through a lecture on Italian history at Cambridge in England, or that on the evening of the day on which he was admitted to practice in the Supreme Court of the United States he gave a lecture in Washington on

"The Curriculum of the Prophets in Ancient Israel." The man's life is a succession of delightful surprises.

An odd trait of his character is his love for fire. He could easily have been a veritable fire-worshiper instead of an orthodox Christian! He has always loved a blaze, and he says reminiscently that for no single thing was he punished so much when he was a child as for building bonfires. After securing possession, as he did in middle age, of the house where he was born and of a great acreage around it, he had one of the most enjoyable times of his life in tearing down old buildings that needed to be destroyed, in heaping up fallen trees and rubbish, in piling great heaps of wood and setting the great piles ablaze. You see, there is one of the secrets of his strength—he has never lost the capacity for fiery enthusiasm!

Always, too, in these later years he is showing his strength and enthusiasm in a positively noble way. He has for years been a keen sufferer from rheumatism and neuritis, but he has never permitted this to interfere with his work or plans. He makes little of his sufferings, and when he slowly makes his way, bent and twisted, downstairs, he does not want to be noticed. "I'm all right," he will say if anyone offers to help, and at such a time comes his nearest approach to impatience. He wants his suffering ignored. Strength has always been to him so precious a belonging that he will not relinquish it while he lives.

"I'm all right!" And he makes himself believe that he is all right even though the pain becomes so severe as to demand massage. He will still, even when suffering, talk calmly, or write his letters, or attend to whatever matters come before him. It is the Spartan boy hiding the pain of the gnawing fox. He never has let pain interfere with his presence on the pulpit or the platform. He has once in a while gone to a meeting on crutches and then, by the force of will, and inspired by what he is to do, has stood before his audience or congregation, a man full of strength and fire and life.

7

How a University Was Founded

The story of the foundation and rise of Temple University is an extraordinary story; it is not only extraordinary, but inspiring; it is not only inspiring, but full of romance.

For the university came out of nothing!—nothing but the need of a young man and the fact that he told the need to one who, throughout his life, has felt the impulse to help anyone in need and has always obeyed the impulse.

I asked Dr. Conwell, up at his home in the Berkshires, to tell me himself just how the university began, and he said that it began because it was needed, and succeeded because of the loyal work of the teachers. When I asked for details, he was silent for a while, looking off into the brooding twilight as it lay over the waters and the trees and the hills, and then he said:

"It was all so simple; it all came about so naturally. One evening, after a service, a young man of the congregation came to me and I saw that he was disturbed about something. I had him sit down by me, and I knew that in a few moments he would tell me what was troubling him.

"'Dr. Conwell,' he said, abruptly, 'I earn but little money, and I see no immediate chance of earning more. I have to support not only myself, but my mother. It leaves nothing at all. Yet my longing is to be a minister. It is the one ambition of my life. Is there anything that I can do?'

"'Any man,' I said to him, 'with the proper determination and ambition can study sufficiently at night to win his desire.'

"'I have tried to think so,' said he, 'but I have not been able to see anything clearly. I want to study, and am ready to give every spare minute to it, but I don't know how to get at it.'

"I thought a few minutes, as I looked at him. He was strong in his desire and in his ambition to fulfill it—strong enough physically and mentally, for work of the body and of the mind—and he needed something more than generalizations of sympathy.

"'Come to me one evening a week and I will begin teaching you myself,' I said, 'and at least you will in that way make a beginning'; and I named the evening.

"His face brightened and he eagerly said that he would come, and left me, but in a little while he came hurrying back again. 'May I bring a friend with me?' he said.

"I told him to bring as many as he wanted to, for more than one would be an advantage, and when the evening came there were six friends with him. That first evening I began to teach them the foundations of Latin."

He stopped as if the story were over. He was looking out thoughtfully into the waning light, and I knew that his mind was busy with those days of the beginning of the institution he so loves, and whose continued success means so much to him. In a little while he went on:

"That was the beginning of it, and there is little more to tell. By the third evening the number of pupils had increased to forty; others joined in helping me, and a room was hired; then a little house, then a second house. From a few students and teachers we became a college. After a while our building went up on Broad Street alongside the Temple Church, and after another while we became a university. From the first our aim"—(I noticed how quickly it had become "our" instead of "my")—"our aim was to give education to those who were unable to get it through the usual channels. And so that was really all there was to it.'

That was typical of Russell Conwell—to tell with brevity of what he has done, to point out the beginnings of something, and quite omit to elaborate as to the results. And that, when you come to know him, is precisely what he means you to understand—that **it is the beginning of anything that is important,** and that if a thing is but earnestly begun and set going in the right way it may just as easily develop big results as little results.

But his story was very far indeed from being "all there was to it," for he had quite omitted to state the extraordinary fact that, beginning with those seven pupils, coming to his library on an evening in 1884, the Temple University has numbered, up to Commencement time in 1915, 88,821 students! Nearly one hundred thousand students, and in the lifetime of the founder! Really, the magnitude of such a work cannot be exaggerated, nor the vast importance of it when it is considered that most of these eighty-eight thousand students would not have received their education had it not been for Temple University. And it all came from the instant response of Russell Conwell to the immediate need presented by a young man without money!

"And there is something else I want to say," said Dr. Conwell, unexpectedly. "I want to say, more fully than a mere casual word, how nobly the work was taken up by volunteer helpers. Professors from the University of Pennsylvania and teachers from the public schools and other local institutions gave freely of what time they could until the new venture was firmly on its way. I honor those who came so devotedly to help. It should be remembered that in those early days, the need was even greater than it would now appear, for there were then no night schools or manual training schools. Since then, the city of Philadelphia has gone into such work, and as fast as it has taken up certain branches the Temple University has put its energy into the branches just higher. And there seems no lessening of the need of it," he added, ponderingly.

No; there is certainly no lessening of the need of it! The figures of the annual catalogue would alone show that.

As early as 1887, just three years after the beginning, the Temple College, as it was by that time called, issued its first catalogue, which set forth with stirring words that the intent of its founding was to:

"Provide such instruction as shall be best adapted to the higher education of those who are compelled to labor at their trade while engaged in study.

"Cultivate a taste for the higher and most useful branches of learning.

"Awaken in the character of young laboring men and women a determined ambition to be useful to their fellow men."

The college—the university as it in time came to be—early broadened its scope, but it has from the first continued to aim at the needs of those unable to secure education without such help as, through its methods, it affords.

It was chartered in 1888, at which time its numbers had reached almost six hundred, and it has ever since had a constant flood of applicants.

"It has demonstrated," as Dr. Conwell puts it, "that those who work for a living have time for study." And he, though he does not himself add this, has given the opportunity.

He feels especial pride in the features by which lectures and recitations are held at practically any hour which best suits the convenience of the students. If any ten students join in a request for any hour from nine in the morning to ten at night a class is arranged for them, to meet that request! This involves the necessity for a much larger number of professors and teachers than would otherwise be necessary, but that is deemed a slight consideration in comparison with the immense good done by meeting the needs of workers.

Also, President Conwell—for of course he is the president of the university—is proud of the fact that the privilege of graduation depends entirely upon knowledge gained; that graduation does not depend upon having listened to any set number of lectures or upon having attended for so many terms or years. If a student can do four years' work in two years or in three he is encouraged to do it, and if he cannot even do it in four he can have no diploma.

Obviously, there is no place at Temple University for students who care only for a few years of leisured ease. It is a place for workers, and not at all for those who merely wish to be able to boast that they attended a university. The students have come largely from among railroad clerks, bank clerks, bookkeepers, teachers, preachers, mechanics, salesmen, drug clerks, city and United States government employees, widows, nurses, housekeepers, brakemen, firemen, engineers, motormen, conductors, and shop hands.

It was when the college became strong enough, and sufficiently advanced in scholarship and standing, and broad enough in scope, to win the name of university, that this title was official granted to it by the State of Pennsylvania, in 1907, and now its educational plan includes three distinct school systems.

First: it offers a high school education to the student who has to quit school after leaving the grammar school.

Second: it offers a full college education, with the branches taught in long-established high grade colleges, to the student who has to quit on leaving the high school.

Third: it offers further scientific or professional education to the college graduate who must go to work immediately on quitting college, but who wishes to take up some such course as law or medicine or engineering.

Out of last year's enrollment of 3,654 it is interesting to notice that the law claimed 141; theology, 182; medicine and pharmacy and dentistry combined, 357; civil engineering, 37; also that the teachers' college, with normal courses on such subjects as household arts and science, kindergarten work, and physical education, took 174; and still more interesting, in a way, to see that 269 students were enrolled for the technical and vocational courses, such as cooking and dressmaking, millinery, manual crafts, school gardening, and storytelling. There were 511 in high school work, and 243 in elementary education. There were 79 studying music, and 68 studying to be trained nurses. There were 606 in the college of liberal arts and sciences, and in the department of commercial education there were 987—for it is a university that offers both scholarship and practicality.

Temple University is not in the least a charitable institution. Its fees are low, and its hours are for the convenience of the students themselves, but it is a place of absolute independence. It is, indeed, a place of far greater independence, so one of the professors pointed out, than are the great universities which receive millions and millions of money in private gifts and endowments.

Temple University in its early years was sorely in need of money, and often there were thrills of expectancy when some man of mighty wealth seemed on the point of giving. But not a single one ever did, and now the Temple likes to feel that it is glad of it. The Temple, to quote its own words, is "An institution for strong men and women who can labor with both mind and body."

The management is proud to be able to say that, although great numbers have come from distant places, "not one of the many thousands ever failed to find an opportunity to support himself."

Even in the early days, when money was needed for the necessary buildings (the buildings of which Conwell dreamed when he left second-story doors in his church!), the university—college it was then called—had won devotion from those who knew that it was a place where neither time nor money was wasted, and where idleness was a crime, and in the donations for the work were many such items as four hundred dollars from factory workers who gave fifty cents each, and two thousand dollars from policemen who gave a dollar each. Within two or three years past the State of Pennsylvania has begun giving it a large sum annually, and this state aid is public recognition of Temple University as an institution of high public value. The state money is invested in the brains and hearts of the ambitious.

So eager is Dr. Conwell to place the opportunity of education before everyone, that even his servants must go to school! He is not one of those who can see needs that are far away but not those that are right at home. **His belief in education, and in the highest attainable education, is profound, and it is not only on account of the abstract pleasure and value of education, but its power of increasing actual earning power and thus making a worker of more value to both himself and the community.**

Many a man and many a woman, while continuing to work for some firm or factory, has taken Temple technical courses and thus fitted himself or herself for an advanced position with the same employer. The Temple knows of many such, who have thus won prominent advancement. And it knows of teachers who, while continuing to teach, have fitted themselves through the Temple courses for professorships. And it knows of many a case of the rise of a Temple student that reads like an Arabian Nights' fancy!—of advance from bookkeeper to editor, from office boy to bank president, from kitchen maid to school principal, from street cleaner to mayor! The Temple University helps them that help themselves.

President Conwell told me personally of one case that especially interested him because it seemed to exhibit, in especial degree, the Temple possibilities. It particularly interested me because it also showed, in high degree, the methods and personality of Dr. Conwell himself.

One day a young woman came to him and said she earned only three dollars a week and that she desired very much to make more. "Can you tell me how to do it?" she said.

He liked her ambition and her directness, but there was something that he felt doubtful about, and that was that her hat looked too expensive for a girl who earned only three dollars a week!

Now, Dr. Conwell is a man whom you would never suspect of giving a thought to the hat of man or woman! But, as a matter of fact, there is very little that he does not see.

Although the hat seemed too expensive for a girl on that low income, Dr. Conwell is not a man who makes snap judgments harshly, and in particular he would be the last man to turn away hastily one who had sought him out for help. He never felt, nor could possibly urge upon anyone, contentment with a humble lot; he stands for advancement; he has no sympathy with that dictum of the smug, that has come to us from a nation tight bound for centuries by its gentry and aristocracy, about being contented with the position in which God has placed you, for he points out that the Bible itself holds up advancement and success as things desirable.

As to the young woman before him, it developed, through discreet inquiry veiled by frank discussion of her case, that she had made the expensive-looking hat herself! Now, not only did all doubtfulness and hesitation vanish, but he saw at once how she could better herself. He knew that a woman who could make a hat like that for herself could make hats for other people, and so, "Go into millinery as a business," he advised.

"Oh—if I only could!" she exclaimed. "But I know that I don't know enough."

"Take the millinery course in Temple University," he responded.

She had not even heard of such a course, and when he went on to explain how she could take it and at the same time continue at her present work until the course was concluded, she was positively ecstatic—it was all so unexpected, this opening of the view of a new and broader life.

"She was an unusual woman," concluded Dr. Conwell, "and she worked with enthusiasm and tirelessness. She graduated, went to an up-state city that seemed to offer a good field, opened a millinery establishment there, with her own name above the door, and became prosperous. That was only a few years ago. And recently I had a letter from her, telling me that last year she netted a clear profit of three thousand six hundred dollars!"

I remember a man, himself of distinguished position, saying of Dr. Conwell, "It is difficult to speak in tempered language of what he has achieved." That just expresses it; the temptation is constantly to use superlatives—for superlatives fit! Of course he has succeeded for himself, and succeeded marvelously, in his rise from the rocky hill farm, but he has done so vastly more than that in inspiring such hosts of others to succeed.!

A dreamer of dreams and a seer of visions—and what realizations have come! And it interested me profoundly not long ago, when Dr. Conwell, talking of the university, unexpectedly remarked that he would like to see such institutions scattered throughout every state in the Union. "All carried on at slight expense to the students and at hours to suit all sorts of working men and women," he added, after a pause; and then, abruptly, **"I should like to see the possibility of higher education offered to everyone in the United States who works for a living."**

There was something superb in the very imagining of such a nationwide system. But I did not ask whether or not he had planned any details for such an effort. I knew that thus far it might only be one of his dreams—but I also knew that his dreams had a way of becoming realities. I had a fleeting glimpse of his soaring vision. **It was amazing to find a man of more than three score and ten thus dreaming of more worlds to conquer.** And I thought, what could the world have accomplished if Methuselah had been a Conwell!—or, far better, what wonders could be accomplished if Conwell could but be a Methuselah and live 969 years, as did the old patriarch!

He has all his life been a great traveler. He is a man who sees vividly and who can describe vividly. Yet often his letters, even from places of the most profound interest, are mostly concerned with affairs back home. It is not that he does not feel, and feel intensely, the interest of what he is visiting, but that his tremendous earnestness keeps him always concerned about his work at home. There could be no stronger example than what I noticed in a letter he wrote from Jerusalem. "I am in Jerusalem! And here at Gethsemane and at the Tomb of Christ." Reading thus far, one expects that any man, and especially a minister, is sure to say something regarding the associations of the place and the effect of these associations on his mind, but Conwell is always the man who is different. "And here at Gethsemane and at the Tomb of Christ, I pray especially for the Temple University." That is Conwellism!

That he founded a hospital—a work in itself great enough for even a great life—is but one among the striking incidents of his career, and it came about through perfect naturalness. He came to know, through his pastoral work and through his growing acquaintance with the needs of the city, that there was a vast amount of suffering and wretchedness and anguish, because of the inability of the existing hospitals to care for all who needed care. There was so much sickness and suffering to be alleviated, there were so many deaths that could have been prevented—and so he decided to start another hospital.

Like everything with him, the beginning was small. That cannot too strongly be set down as the way of this phenomenally successful organizer. Most men would have to wait until a big beginning could be made, and so would most likely never make a beginning at all. But Conwell's way is to dream of future bigness, but be ready to begin at once, no matter how small or insignificant the beginning may appear to others.

Two rented rooms, one nurse, one patient—this was the humble beginning, in 1891, of what has developed into the great Samaritan Hospital. In a year there was an entire house, fitted up with wards and operating room. Now it occupies several buildings, including and adjoining that first one, and a great new structure is planned. But even as it is, it has a hundred and seventy beds, is fitted with all modern hospital appliances, and has a large staff of physicians, and the number of surgical operations performed there is very large.

It is open to sufferers of any race or creed, and the poor are never refused admission, the rule being that treatment is free for those who cannot pay, but that such as can afford it shall pay according to their means.

The hospital has a kindly feature that endears it to patients and their relatives alike. It is that, by Dr. Conwell's personal order, there are not only the usual weekday hours for visiting, but also one evening a week and every Sunday afternoon. "For otherwise," as he says, "many would be unable to come because they could not get away from their work."

A little over eight years ago another hospital was taken in charge, the Garretson—not founded by Conwell, this one, but acquired, and promptly expanded in its usefulness.

Both the Samaritan and the Garretson are part of Temple University. The Samaritan Hospital has treated, since its foundation, up to the middle of 1915, 29,301 patients; the Garretson, in its shorter life, 5,923. Including dispensary cases as well as house patients, the two hospitals together, under the headship of President Conwell, have handled over 400,000 cases.

How Conwell can possibly meet the multifarious demands upon his time is in itself a miracle. He is the head of the great church; he is the head of the university; he is the head of the hospitals; he is the head of everything with which he is associated! And he is not only nominally, but very actively, the head!

8

His Splendid Efficiency

Conwell has a few strong and efficient executive helpers who have long been associated with him—men
and women who know his ideas and ideals, who are devoted to him, and who do their utmost to relieve him, and,
of course, there is very much that is thus done for him.
However, he is so overshadowing a man (there is really no
other word) that all who work with him look to him for
advice and guidance—the professors and the students, the
doctors and the nurses, the church officers, the Sunday
school teachers, the members of his congregation. He is
never too busy to see anyone who really wishes to see him.

**He can attend to a vast intricacy of detail, and an-
swer myriad personal questions and doubts, and keep
the great institutions splendidly going, by thorough sys-
tematization of time, and by watching every minute.** He
has several secretaries, for special work, besides his private
secretary. His correspondence is very great. Often he dic-
tates to a secretary as he travels on the train. Even in the
few days for which he can run back to the Berkshires, work
is awaiting him. Work follows him. After knowing of this,
one is positively amazed that he is able to give to his coun-
try-wide lectures the time and the traveling that they in-
exorably demand. Only a man of immense strength, of the
greatest stamina, a veritable superman, could possibly do

it. At times one quite forgets, noticing the multiplicity of his occupations, that he prepares two sermons and two talks on every Sunday!

Here is his usual Sunday schedule, when at home. He rises at seven and studies until breakfast, which is at eight-thirty. Then he studies until nine forty-five, when he leads a men's meeting at which he is likely also to play the organ and lead the singing. At ten-thirty is the principal church service, at which he preaches, and at the close of which he shakes hands with hundreds. He dines at one, after which he takes fifteen minutes' rest and then reads. At three o'clock he addresses, in a talk that is like another sermon, a large class of men—not the same men as in the morning. He is also sure to look in at the regular session of the Sunday school. Home again, where he studies and reads until suppertime. At seven-thirty is the evening service, at which he again preaches and after which he shakes hands with several hundred more and talks personally, in his study, with any who have need of talk with him. He is usually home by ten-thirty. I spoke of it, one evening, as having been a strenuous day, and he responded, with a cheerfully whimsical smile: "Three sermons and shook hands with nine hundred."

That evening, as the service closed, he had said to the congregation: "I shall be here for an hour. We always have a pleasant time together after service. If you are acquainted with me, come up and shake hands. If you are strangers"—just the slightest of pauses—"come up and let us make an acquaintance that will last for eternity." I remember how simply and easily this was said, in his clear, deep voice, and how impressive and important it seemed, and with what unexpectedness it came. **"Come and make an acquaintance that will last for eternity!"** And there was a serenity about his way of saying this which would make strangers think—just as he meant them to think—that he had nothing whatever to do but to talk with them. Even his own congregation have, most of them, little conception of how busy a man he is and how precious is his time.

One evening last June—to take an evening of which I happened to know—he got home from a journey of two hundred miles at six o'clock, and after dinner and a slight rest went to the church prayer meeting, which he led in his usual vigorous way at such meetings, playing the organ and leading the singing, as well as praying and talking. After the prayer meeting he went to two dinners in succession, both of them important dinners in connection with the close of the university year, and at both dinners he spoke. At the second dinner he was notified of the sudden illness of a member of his congregation, and instantly hurried to the man's home and thence to the hospital to which he had been removed, and there he remained at the man's bedside, or in consultation with the physicians, until one in the morning. He was up at seven and again at work.

"This one thing I do," is his private maxim of efficiency, and a literalist might point out that he does not one thing only, but a thousand things, not getting Conwell's meaning, which is that **whatever the thing may be which he is doing, he lets himself think of nothing else until it is done.**

Dr. Conwell has a profound love for the country and particularly for the country of his own youth. He loves the wind that comes sweeping over the hills, he loves the wide-stretching views from the heights and the forest intimacies of the nestled nooks. He loves the rippling streams, he loves the wild flowers that nestle in seclusion or that unexpectedly paint some mountain meadow with delight. He loves the very touch of the earth, and he loves the great bare rocks.

He writes verses at times; he has written lines for a few old tunes. It interested me greatly to chance upon some lines of his that picture heaven in terms of the Berkshires:

The wide-stretching valleys in colors so fadeless,
Where trees are all deathless and flowers e'er bloom.

That is heaven in the eyes of a New England hillman! Not golden pavement and ivory palaces, but valleys and trees and flowers and the wide sweep of the open.

Few things please him more than to go, for example, blackberrying, and he has a knack of never scratching his face or his fingers when doing so. And he finds blackberrying, whether he goes alone or with friends, an extraordinarily good time for planning something he wishes to do or working out the thought of a sermon. Fishing is even better, for in fishing he finds immense recreation and restfulness and at the same time a further opportunity to think and plan.

As a small boy he wished that he could throw a dam across the trout brook that runs near the little Conwell home, and—as he never gives up—he finally realized the ambition, although it was after half a century! And now he has a big pond, three quarters of a mile long by half a mile wide, lying in front of the house, down a slope from it—a pond stocked with splendid pickerel. He likes to float about restfully on this pond, thinking or fishing, or both. And on that pond he showed me how to catch pickerel even under a blaze of sunlight!

He is a trout fisher, too, for it is a trout stream that feeds this pond and goes dashing away from it through the wilderness. For miles adjoining his place a fishing club of wealthy men bought up the rights in this trout stream, and they approached him with a liberal offer. But he declined it.

"I remembered what good times I had when I was a boy, fishing up and down that stream, and I couldn't think of keeping the boys of the present day from such a pleasure. So they may still come and fish for trout here."

As we walked one day beside this brook, he suddenly said: "Did you ever notice that every brook has its own song? I should know the song of this brook anywhere."

It would seem as if he loved his rugged native country because it is rugged even more than because it is native! Himself so rugged, so hardy, so enduring—the strength of the hills is his also.

Always, in his very appearance, you see something of this ruggedness of the hills: a ruggedness, a sincerity, a plainness, that mark alike his character and his looks. Always one realizes the strength of the man, even when his voice, as it usually is, is low. One increasingly realizes the strength when, on the lecture platform or in the pulpit or in conversation, he flashes vividly into fire.

A big-boned man he is, sturdy-framed, a tall man, with broad shoulders and strong hands. His hair is a deep chestnut brown that at first sight seems black. In his early manhood he was superb in looks, as his pictures show, but anxiety and work and the constant flight of years, with physical pain, have settled his face into lines of sadness and almost of severity, which instantly vanish when he speaks. His face is illumined by marvelous eyes.

He is a lonely man. The wife of his early years died long, long ago, before success had come, and she was deeply mourned, for she had loyally helped him through a time that held much of struggle and hardship. He married again, and this wife was his loyal helpmate for many years. In a time of special stress, when an embezzlement of sixty-five thousand dollars threatened to crush Temple College just when it was getting on its feet, for both Temple Church and Temple College had in those early days buoyantly assumed heavy indebtedness, he raised every dollar he could by selling or mortgaging his own possessions, and in this his wife, as he lovingly remembers, most cordially stood beside him, although she knew that if anything should happen to him the financial sacrifice would leave her penniless. She died after years of companionship; his children married and made homes of their own; he is a lonely man. Yet he is not unhappy, for the tremendous demands of his tremendous work leave him little time for sadness or retrospect. At times the realization comes that he is getting old, that friends and comrades have been passing away, leaving him an old man with younger friends and helpers. But such realization only makes him work with an earnestness still more intense, knowing that the night cometh when no man shall work.

Deeply religious though he is, he does not force religion into conversation on ordinary subjects or upon people who may not be interested in it. **With him, it is action and good works, with faith and belief, that count,** except when talk is the natural, the fitting, the necessary thing; when addressing either one individual or thousands, he talks with superb effectiveness.

His sermons are, it may almost literally be said, parable after parable, although he himself would be the last man to say this, for it would sound as if he claimed to model after the greatest of all examples. His own way of putting it is that he uses stories frequently because people are more impressed by illustrations than by argument.

Always, whether in the pulpit or out of it, he is simple and homelike, human and unaffected. If he happens to see someone in the congregation to whom he wishes to speak, he may just leave his pulpit and walk down the aisle, while the choir is singing, and quietly say a few words and return.

In the early days of his ministry, if he heard of a poor family in immediate need of food, he would be quite likely to gather a basket of provisions and go personally, and offer this assistance and such other as he might find necessary when he reached the place. As he became known, he ceased from this direct and open method of charity, for he knew that impulsiveness would be taken for intentional display. But he has never ceased to be ready to help on the instant that he knows help is needed. Delay and lengthy investigation are avoided by him when he can be certain that something immediate is required. And the extent of his quiet charity is amazing. With no family for which to save money, and with no care to put away money for himself, **he thinks only of money as an instrument for helpfulness.** I never heard a friend criticize him except for too great open-handedness.

I was strongly impressed, after coming to know him, that he possessed many of the qualities that made for the success of the old-time district leaders of New York City. I mentioned this to him, and he at once responded that he had himself met "Big Tim," the long-time leader of the Sullivans, and had had him at his house, Big Tim having gone to Philadelphia to aid some henchman in trouble, and having promptly sought the aid of Dr. Conwell. It was characteristic of Conwell that he saw what so many never saw, the most striking characteristic of that Tammany leader. For, "Big Tim Sullivan was so kind-hearted!" Conwell appreciated the man's political unscrupulousness as well as did his enemies, but he saw also what made his underlying power—his kind-heartedness. Except that Sullivan could be supremely unscrupulous, and that Conwell is supremely scrupulous, there were marked similarities in these masters over men. Conwell possesses, as Sullivan possessed, a wonderful memory for faces and names.

Naturally, Russell Conwell stands steadily and strongly for good citizenship. But he never talks boastful Americanism. He seldom speaks in so many words of either Americanism or good citizenship, but he constantly and silently keeps the American flag, as the symbol of good citizenship, before his people. An American flag is prominent in his church; an American flag is seen in his home; a beautiful American flag is up at his Berkshire place and surmounts a lofty tower where, when he was a boy, there stood a mighty tree at the top of which was an eagle's nest, which has given him a name for his home, for he terms it "The Eagle's Nest."

Remembering a long story that I had read of his climbing to the top of that tree, though it was a well-nigh impossible feat, and securing the nest by great perseverance and daring, I asked him if the story were a true one. "Oh, I've heard something about it; somebody said that somebody watched me, or something of the kind. But I don't remember anything about it myself."

Any friend of his is sure to say something, after a while, about his determination, his insistence on going ahead with anything on which he has really set his heart. One of the very important things on which he insisted, in spite of very great opposition, and especially an opposition from the other churches of this denomination (for this was a good many years ago, when there was much more narrowness in churches and sects than there is at present), was with regard to doing away with close communion. He determined on an open communion, and his way of putting it, once decided upon, was: "My friends, it is not for me to invite you to the table of the Lord. The table of the Lord is open. If you feel that you can come to the table, it is open to you." And this is the form which he still uses.

He not only never gives up, but, so his friends say, **he never forgets a thing upon which he has once decided,** and at times, long after they supposed the matter has been entirely forgotten, they suddenly find Dr. Conwell bringing his original purpose to pass. When I was told of this I remembered that pickerel pond in the Berkshires!

If he is really set upon doing anything, little or big, adverse criticism does not disturb his serenity. Some years ago he began wearing a huge diamond, whose size attracted much criticism and caustic comment. He never said a word in defense; he just kept on wearing the diamond. One day, however, after some years, he took it off, and people said, "He has listened to the criticism at last!" He smiled reminiscently as he told me about this, and said: "A dear old deacon of my congregation gave me that diamond and I did not like to hurt his feelings by refusing it. It really bothered me to wear such a glaring big thing, but because I didn't want to hurt the old deacon's feelings I kept on wearing it until he was dead. Then I stopped wearing it."

The ambition of Russell Conwell is to continue working and working until the very last moment of his life. In work he forgets his sadness, his loneliness, his age. He said to me one day, "I will die in harness."

9

The Story of "Acres of Diamonds"

Considering everything, the most remarkable thing in Russell Conwell's remarkable life is his lecture, "Acres of Diamonds." That is, the lecture itself, the number of times he has delivered it, what a source of inspiration it has been to myriads, the money that he has made and is making, and, still more, the purpose to which he directs the money. In the circumstances surrounding "Acres of Diamonds," in its tremendous success, in the attitude of mind revealed by the lecture itself and by what Dr. Conwell does with it, it is illuminative of his character, his aims, his ability.

The lecture is vibrant with his energy. It flashes with his hopefulness. It is full of his enthusiasm. It is packed full of his intensity. **It stands for the possibilities of success in everyone.** He has delivered it over six thousand times. The demand for it never diminishes. The success grows never less.

There is a time in Russell Conwell's youth of which it is pain for him to think. He told me of it one evening, and his voice sank lower and lower as he went far back into the past. It was of his days at Yale that he spoke, for they were days of suffering, for he had not money for Yale, and in working for more he endured bitter humiliation. It was not that the work was hard, for Russell Conwell has always been ready for hard work. It was not that there were privations and difficulties, for he has always found difficulties only things to overcome, and endured privations with cheerful fortitude. But it was the humiliations that he met—the personal humiliations that after more than half a century make him suffer in remembering them—yet out of those humiliations came a marvelous result.

"I determined," he says, "that whatever I could do to make the way easier at college for other young men working their way I would do."

And so, many years ago, he began to devote every dollar that he made from "Acres of Diamonds" to this definite purpose. He has what may be termed a waiting list. On that list are very few cases he has looked into personally. Infinitely busy man that he is, he cannot do extensive personal investigation. A large proportion of his names come to him from college presidents who know of students in their own colleges in need of such a helping hand.

"Every night," he said, when I asked him to tell me about it, "when my lecture is over and the check is in my hand, I sit down in my room in the hotel"—what a lonely picture, too!—"I sit down in my room in the hotel and subtract from the total sum received my actual expenses for that place, and make out a check for the difference and send it to some young man on my list. And I always send with the check a letter of advice and helpfulness, expressing my hope that it will be of some service to him and telling him that he is to feel under no obligation except to his Lord. I feel strongly, and I try to make every young man feel, that there must be no sense of obligation to me personally. And I tell them that I am hoping to leave behind me men who will do more work than I have done. Don't think that I put in too much advice," he added, with a smile, "for I only try to let them know that a friend is trying to help them."

His face lighted as he spoke. "There is such a fascination in it!" he exclaimed. "It is just like a gamble! And as soon as I have sent the letter and crossed a name off my list, I am aiming for the next one!"

After a pause he added: "I do not attempt to send any young man enough for all his expenses. But I want to save him from bitterness, and each check will help. And, too," he concluded, naively, in the vernacular, "I don't want them to lay down on me!"

He told me that he made it clear that he did not wish to get returns or reports from this branch of his lifework, for it would take a great deal of time in watching and thinking and in the reading and writing of letters. "But it is mainly," he went on, "that I do not wish to hold over their heads the sense of obligation."

When I suggested that this was surely an example of bread cast upon the waters that could not return, he was silent for a little and then said, thoughtfully: **"As one gets on in years there is satisfaction in doing a thing for the sake of doing it. The bread returns in the sense of effort made."**

On a recent trip through Minnesota he was positively upset, so his secretary told me, through being recognized on a train by a young man who had been helped through "Acres of Diamonds," and who, finding that this was really Dr. Conwell, eagerly brought his wife to join him in most fervent thanks for his assistance. Both the husband and his wife were so emotionally overcome that it quite overcame Dr. Conwell himself.

The lecture, to quote the noble words of Dr. Conwell himself, is designed to help "every person, of either sex, who cherishes the high resolve of sustaining a career of usefulness and honor." It is a lecture of helpfulness. And it is a lecture, when given with Conwell's voice and face and manner, that is full of fascination. And yet it is all so simple!

It is packed full of inspiration, of suggestion, of aid. He alters it to meet the local circumstances of the thousands of different places in which he delivers it. But the base remains the same. And even those to whom it is an old story will go to hear him time after time. It amuses him to say that he knows individuals who have listened to it twenty times.

It begins with a story told to Conwell by an old Arab as the two journeyed together toward Nineveh, and, as you listen, you hear the actual voices and you see the sands of the desert and the waving palms. The lecturer's voice is so easy, so effortless, it seems so ordinary and matter-of-fact—yet the entire scene is instantly vital and alive! Instantly the man has his audience under a sort of spell, eager to listen, ready to be merry or grave. He has the faculty of control, the vital quality that makes the orator.

The same people will go to hear this lecture over and over, and that is the kind of tribute that Conwell likes. I recently heard him deliver it in his own church, where it would naturally be thought to be an old story, and where, presumably, only a few of the faithful would go, but it was quite clear that all of his church are the faithful, for it was a large audience that came to listen to him; hardly a seat in the great auditorium was vacant. It should be added that, although it was in his own church, it was not a free lecture, where a throng might be expected, but that each one paid a liberal sum for a seat—and the paying of admission is always a practical test of the sincerity of desire to hear. And the people were swept along by the current as if lecturer and lecture were of novel interest. The lecture in itself is good to read, but it is only when it is illumined by

Conwell's vivid personality that one understands how it influences in the actual delivery.

On that particular evening he had decided to give the lecture in the same form as when he first delivered it many years ago, without any of the alterations that have come with time and changing localities. As he went on, with the audience rippling and bubbling with laughter as usual, he never doubted that he was giving it as he had given it years before. Yet so up-to-date and alive must he necessarily be, in spite of a definite effort to set himself back—every once in a while he was coming out with illustrations from such distinctly recent things as the automobile!

The last time I heard him was the 5,124th time for the lecture. Doesn't it seem incredible! 5,124 times! I noticed that he was to deliver it at a little out-of-the-way place, difficult for any considerable number to get to, and I wondered just how much of an audience would gather and how they would be impressed. So I went over from where I was, a few miles away. The road was dark and I pictured a small audience, but when I got there I found the church building in which he was to deliver the lecture had a seating capacity of 830 and that precisely 830 people were already seated there and that a fringe of others were standing behind. Many had come from miles away, yet the lecture had scarcely, if at all, been advertised. But people had said to one another: "Aren't you going to hear Dr. Conwell?" And the word had thus been passed along.

I remember how fascinating it was to watch that audience, for they responded so keenly and with such heartfelt pleasure throughout the entire lecture. Not only were they immensely pleased and amused and interested—and to achieve that at a crossroads church was in itself a triumph to be proud of—but I knew that every listener was given an impulse toward doing something for himself and for others, and that with at least some of them the impulse would materialize in acts. Over and over one realizes what a power such a man wields.

And what an unselfishness! For, far on in years as he is, and suffering pain, he does not chop down his lecture to a definite length. He does not talk for just an hour or go on grudgingly for an hour and a half. He sees that the people are fascinated and inspired, and he forgets pain, ignores time, forgets that the night is late and that he has a long journey to go to get home, and keeps on generously for two hours! And everyone wishes it were four.

Always he talks with ease and sympathy. There are geniality, composure, humor, simple and homely jests— yet never does the audience forget that he is every moment in tremendous earnest. They bubble with responsive laughter or are silent in riveted attention. A stir can be seen to sweep over an audience, of earnestness or surprise or amusement or resolve. When he is grave and sober or fervid the people feel that he is himself a fervidly earnest man, and when he is telling something humorous there is on his part almost a repressed chuckle, a genial appreciation of the fun of it, not in the least as if he were laughing at his own humor, but as if he and his hearers were laughing together at something of which they were all humorously cognizant.

Myriad successes in life have come through the direct inspiration of this single lecture. One hears of so many that there must be vastly more that are never told. A few of the most recent were told me by Dr. Conwell himself, one being of a farmer boy who walked a long distance to hear him. On his way home, so the boy, now a man, has written him, he thought over and over of what he could do to advance himself, and before he reached home he learned that a teacher was wanted at a certain country school. He knew he did not know enough to teach, but was sure he could learn, so he bravely asked for the place. And something in his earnestness made him win a temporary appointment. Thereupon he worked and studied so hard and so devotedly, while he daily taught, that within a few months he was regularly employed there. "And now," says Conwell, abruptly, with his characteristic skimming over of the intermediate details between the important beginning of a thing and the satisfactory end, "and now that young man is one of our college presidents."

Very recently, a lady came to Dr. Conwell, the wife of an exceptionally prominent man who was earning a large salary, and she told him that her husband was so unselfishly generous with money that often they were almost in straits. She said they had bought a little farm as a country place, paying only a few hundred dollars for it, and that she had said to herself, laughingly, after hearing the lecture, "There are no acres of diamonds on this place!" But she also went on to tell that she had found a spring of exceptionally fine water there, although in buying they had scarcely known of the spring at all. She had been so inspired by Conwell that she had had the water analyzed and, finding that it was remarkably pure, had begun to have it bottled and sold under a trade name as special spring water. And she is making money. She also sells pure ice from the pool, cut in wintertime—and all because of "Acres of Diamonds"!

Several millions of dollars in all, have been received by Russell Conwell as the proceeds from this single lecture. Such a fact is almost staggering—and it is more staggering to realize what good is done in the world by this man, who does not earn for himself, but uses his money in immediate helpfulness. And one can neither think nor write with moderation when it is further realized that far more good than can be done directly with money he does by uplifting and inspiring with this lecture. Always his heart is with the weary and the heavy laden. Always he stands for self-betterment.

Last year, 1914, he and his work were given unique recognition. It was known by his friends that this particular lecture was approaching its five-thousandth delivery, and they planned a celebration of such an event in the history of the most popular lecture in the world. Dr. Conwell agreed to deliver it in the Academy of Music, in Philadelphia, and the building was packed and the streets outside were thronged. The proceeds from all sources for that five-thousandth lecture were over nine thousand dollars.

The hold which Russell Conwell has gained on the affections and respect of his home city was seen not only in the thousands who strove to hear him, but in the prominent men who served on the local committee in charge of the celebration. There was a national committee, too, and the nationwide love that he has won, the nationwide appreciation of what he has done and is still doing, was shown by the fact that among the names of the notables on this committee were those of nine governors of states. The Governor of Pennsylvania was himself present to do Russell Conwell honor, and he gave to him a key emblematic of the Freedom of the State.

The "Freedom of the State"—yes; this man, well over seventy, has won it. The Freedom of the State, the Freedom of the Nation—for this man of helpfulness, this marvelous exponent of the gospel of success, has worked marvelously for the freedom, the betterment, the liberation, the advancement, of the individual.

Fifty Years on the Lecture Platform

BY
RUSSELL H. CONWELL

Fifty Years on the Lecture Platform

A n Autobiography! What an absurd request! If all the conditions were favorable, the story of my public life could not be made interesting. It does not seem possible that any will care to read so plain and uneventful a tale. I see nothing in it for boasting, nor much that could be helpful. Then, I never saved a scrap of paper intentionally concerning my work to which I could refer, not a book, not a sermon, not a lecture, not a newspaper notice or account, not a magazine article, not one of the kind biographies written from time to time by noble friends have I ever kept even as a souvenir, although some of them may be in my library. I have ever felt that the writers concerning my life were too generous and that my own work was too hastily done. Hence I have nothing upon which to base an autobiographical account, except the recollections which come to an overburdened mind.

My general view of half a century on the lecture platform brings to me precious and beautiful memories, and fills my soul with devout gratitude for the blessings and kindnesses which have been given to me so far beyond my deserts. So much more success has come to my hands than I ever expected; so much more of good have I found than even youth's wildest dream included; so much more effective have been my weakest endeavors than I ever planned or hoped—that a biography written truthfully would be mostly an account of what men and women have done for me.

I have lived to see accomplished far more than my highest ambition included, and have seen the enterprises I have undertaken rush by me, pushed on by a thousand strong hands until they have left me far behind them. The realities are like dreams to me. Blessings on the loving hearts and noble minds who have been so willing to sacrifice for others' good and to think only of what they could do, and never of what they should get! Many of them have ascended into the Shining Land, and here I am in mine age gazing up alone,

> *Only waiting till the shadows*
> *Are a little longer grown.*

Fifty years! I was a young man, not yet of age, when I delivered my first platform lecture. The Civil War of 1861-65 drew on with all its passions, patriotism, horrors, and fears, and I was studying law at Yale University. I had from childhood felt that I was "called to the ministry." The earliest event of memory is the prayer of my father at family prayers in the little old cottage in the Hampshire highlands of the Berkshire Hills, calling on God with a sobbing voice to lead me into some special service for the Savior. It filled me with awe, dread, and fear, and I recoiled from the thought, until I determined to fight against it with all my power. So I sought for other professions and for decent excuses for being anything but a preacher.

Yet while I was nervous and timid before the class in declamation and dreaded to face any kind of an audience, I felt in my soul a strange impulse toward public speaking which for years made me miserable. The war and the public meetings for recruiting soldiers furnished an outlet for my suppressed sense of duty, and my first lecture was on the "Lessons of History" as applied to the campaigns against the Confederacy.

That matchless temperance orator and loving friend, John B. Gough, introduced me to the little audience in Westfield, Massachusetts, in 1862. What a foolish little schoolboy speech it must have been! But Mr. Gough's kind words of praise, the bouquets and the applause, made me feel that somehow the way to public oratory would not be so hard as I had feared.

From that time I acted on Mr. Gough's advice and "sought practice" by accepting almost every invitation I received to speak on any kind of a subject. There were many sad failures and tears, but it was a restful compromise with my conscience concerning the ministry, and it pleased my friends. I addressed picnics, Sunday schools, patriotic meetings, funerals, anniversaries, commencements, debates, cattle shows, and sewing circles without partiality and without price. For the first five years the income was all experience. Then voluntary gifts began to come occasionally in the shape of a jackknife, a ham, a book, and the first cash remuneration was from a farmers' club, of seventy-five cents toward the "horse hire." It was a curious fact that one member of that club afterward moved to Salt Lake City and was a member of the committee at the Mormon Tabernacle in 1872 which, when I was a correspondent on a journey around the world, employed me to lecture on "Men of the Mountains" in the Mormon Tabernacle, at a fee of five hundred dollars.

While I was gaining practice in the first years of platform work, I had the good fortune to have profitable employment as a soldier, or as a correspondent or lawyer, or as an editor or as a preacher, which enabled me to pay my own expenses, and it has been seldom in the fifty years that I have ever taken a fee for my personal use. In the last thirty-six years I have dedicated solemnly all the lecture income to benevolent enterprises. If I am antiquated enough for an autobiography, perhaps I may be aged enough to avoid the criticism of being an egotist, when I state that some years I delivered one lecture, "Acres of Diamonds," over two hundred times each year, at an average income of about one hundred and fifty dollars for each lecture.

It was a remarkable good fortune which came to me as a lecturer when Mr. James Redpath organized the first lecture bureau ever established. Mr. Redpath was the biographer of John Brown of Harper's Ferry renown, and as Mr. Brown had been long a friend of my father's I found employment, while a student on vacation, in selling that life of John Brown. That acquaintance with Mr. Redpath was maintained until Mr. Redpath's death. To General Charles H. Taylor, with whom I was employed for a time as reporter for the Boston *Daily Traveler*, I was indebted for many acts of self-sacrificing friendship which soften my soul as I recall them. He did me the greatest kindness when he suggested my name to Mr. Redpath as one who could "fill in the vacancies in the smaller towns" where the "great lights could not always be secured."

What a glorious galaxy of great names that original list of Redpath lecturers contained! Henry Ward Beecher, John B. Gough, Senator Charles Sumner, Theodore Tilton, Wendell Phillips, Mrs. Mary A. Livermore, Bayard Taylor, Ralph Waldo Emerson, with many of the great preachers, musicians, and writers of that remarkable era. Even Dr. Holmes, John Whittier, Henry W. Longfellow, John Lothrop Motley, George William Curtis, and General Burnside were persuaded to appear one or more times, although they refused to receive pay. I cannot forget how ashamed I felt when my name appeared in the shadow of such names, and how sure I was that every acquaintance was ridiculing me behind my back. Mr. Bayard Taylor, however, wrote me from the *Tribune* office a kind note saying that he was glad to see me "on the road to great usefulness." Governor Clafflin, of Massachusetts, took the time to send me a note of congratulation. General Benjamin F. Butler, however, advised me to "stick to the last" and be a good lawyer.

The work of lecturing was always a task and a duty. I do not feel now that I ever sought to be an entertainer. I am sure I would have been an utter failure but for the feeling that I must preach some gospel truth in my lectures and do at least that much toward that ever-persistent "call of God." When I entered the ministry (1879) I had become so associated with the lecture platform in America and England that I could not feel justified in abandoning so great a field of usefulness.

The experiences of all our successful lecturers are probably nearly alike. The way is not always smooth. However, the hard roads, the poor hotels, the late trains, the cold halls, the hot church auditoriums, the overkindness of hospitable committees, and the broken hours of sleep are annoyances one soon forgets. The hosts of intelligent faces, the messages of thanks, and the effects of the earnings on the lives of young college men can never cease to be a daily joy. God bless them all.

Often have I been asked if I did not, in fifty years of travel in all sorts of conveyances, meet with accidents. It is a marvel to me that no such event ever brought me harm. In a continuous period of over twenty-seven years I delivered about two lectures in every three days, yet I did not miss a single engagement. Sometimes I had to hire a special train, but I reached the town on time, with only a rare exception, and then I was but a few minutes late. Accidents have preceded and followed me on trains and boats, and were sometimes in sight, but I was preserved without injury through all the years. In the Johnstown flood region I saw a bridge go out behind our train. I was once on a derelict steamer on the Atlantic for twenty-six days. At another time a man was killed in the berth of a sleeper I had left half an hour before. Often have I felt the train leave the track, but no one was killed. Robbers have several times threatened my life, but all came out without loss to me. God and man have ever been patient with me.

Yet this period of lecturing has been, after all, a side issue. The Temple, and its church, in Philadelphia, which, when its membership was less than three thousand members, for so many years contributed through its membership over sixty thousand dollars a year for the uplift of humanity, had made life a continual surprise. The Samaritan Hospital's amazing growth, and the Garretson Hospital's dispensaries, have been so continually ministering to the sick and poor, and have done such skillful work for the tens of thousands who ask for their help each year, that I have been made happy while away lecturing by the feeling that each hour and minute they were faithfully doing good. Temple University, which was founded only twenty-seven years ago, has already sent out into a higher income and nobler life nearly a hundred thousand young men and women who could not probably have obtained an education in any other institution. The faithful, self-sacrificing faculty, now numbering two hundred and fifty-three professors, have done the real work. For that I can claim but little credit, and I mention the University here only to show that my "fifty years on the lecture platform" has necessarily been a sideline of work.

My best-known lecture, "Acres of Diamonds," was a mere accidental address, at first given before a reunion of my old comrades of the Forty-sixth Massachusetts Regiment, which served in the Civil War and in which I was captain. I had no thought of giving the address again, and even after it began to be called for by lecture committees I did not dream that I should live to deliver it, as I now have done, five thousand times.

"What is the secret of its popularity?" I could never explain it to myself or others. I simply know that I **always attempt to enthuse myself on each occasion with the idea that it is a special opportunity to do good,** and I interest myself in each community and apply the general principles with local illustrations.

The hand which now holds this pen must in the natural course of events soon cease to gesture on the platform, and **it is a sincere, prayerful hope that this book will go on into the years doing increasing good for the aid of my brothers and sisters in the human family.**

RUSSELL H. CONWELL
South Worthington, Mass.,
September 1, 1913.

Publisher:

Tree of Life Publications

Box 126, Joshua Tree CA 92252

(619) 366-3695 or (800) 247-6553

Free Catalog